BORODINO

DIGBY SMITH

THE WINDRUSH PRESS · GLOUCESTERSHIRE

First published in Great Britain by The Windrush Press, 1998
Little Window, High Street
Moreton-in-Marsh
Gloucestershire GL56 OLL
Tel.: 01608 652012
Fax: 01608 652125
Email: windrush@netcomuk.co.uk

British Library Cataloguing in Publication Data

A catalogue record for this book is available from the British Library

ISBN 1 900624 17 6

Typeset by Archetype IT Ltd, web site http://www.archetype-it.com

Printed and bound in Malta by Interprint Ltd., Malta

The front cover shows a detail from *Battle of Borodino 7 September 1812* by General Baron Lejeune which shows Marshal Berthier returning the sword of General Sokereff (Peter Newarks' Military Pictures)

Cover design by Miranda Harvey

Contents

List of Illustrations,
Maps, and Commanders

Napoleon Bonaparte, Emperor of the French, leaving
Moscow on 19 October 1812
Author's collection

MAPS

COMMANDERS

Foreword

Borodino: this battle, the second-bloodiest of the Napoleonic wars, after Leipzig in 1813, has inspired many books, paintings, and even musical compositions.

It involved a quarter-of-a-million men and over a thousand guns; the casualty lists included (according to some estimates) up to 100,000 men, although this figure is most probably only a French propaganda claim.

Having now studied the battle, in the context of the Russian campaign and the aims of the protagonists – Napoleon Bonaparte, Emperor of the French, on the one hand, and Alexander, Tsar of all the Russias, on the other – I find it to be characterised by four concepts: courage, inertia, waste, and futility.

Courage: the bravery displayed by all participants in the hell of 7 September, regardless of their nationality, is nothing short of astounding. When one reads the dry, sober language of the official reports and the eye-witness accounts, they cannot conceal the superhuman challenges which were repeatedly met and overcome by the generals, officers, NCOs, and common soldiers on both sides.

Inertia: Having issued their orders for the forthcoming battle on 6 September, both commanders-in-chief, Napoleon and Kutuzov, practically withdrew from any hands-on management of the action on the next day. To an extent, of course, this is right and proper. All responsible managers must allow their subordinates to carry out the agreed plan with the minimum interference from above, within certain limits of tolerance.

History has revealed that Napoleon (then forty-two years old) had been suffering from cystitis for some time before the battle of Borodino. This means that he would have been plagued by a constant urge to urinate, but the act of doing so would have caused him acute discomfort, a distraction indeed. This may explain why he reportedly spent so much of the day idly at Shevardino, in contrast to his management style in all his campaigns through 1809 when he was everywhere at once, wearing out horses and ADCs, in the process of controlling all the crucial aspects of the battles on the ground.

History also reveals to us that his opponent, Kutuzov (then sixty-seven), blind in one eye and extremely overweight, had worked long and hard to build a reputation as a commander characterised by inactivity, apparent idleness, and sloth. His supporters claim that, within this convincing cloak of incompetence, there lurked a formidable and cunning foe ready to pounce with lightning speed, as and when needed. The history of the campaign in Russia after Borodino – even as late as the Beresina crossing – reveals no such flashes of genius. At Kutuzov's age, it would have been foolish to expect them.

Kutuzov was an immensely popular choice (with the Russians) to replace the 'foreigner', Barclay de Tolly, who had led the demoralising (but vitally necessary) withdrawal so far. But not everyone in the Russian high command forgot that it was Barclay who had preserved the Russian armies for just such a strategically vital battle.

At Borodino, initiative in the Russian army's actions was rarely shown above corps level.

Waste: owing to the bankruptcy of ideas at the higher levels of command on both sides, there were (with the exception of Uvarov's unexploited raid) no amazing gambits in the game. It was a needlessly bloody slogging match where the lower echelons of each army paid with their lives for the errors and omissions of their commanders. What little remained of Napoleon's cavalry was largely destroyed around the Bagration *Flèches* (a trio of three V-shaped fortifications). It was impossible for him to replace these losses because of the Russian counter-measures.

Futility: coupled with the waste, when one analyses the strategic effects of Borodino, there is a clear and inescapable end result to the whole equation. Despite all the heroism, self-sacrifice, death, suffering, and destruction, it achieved nothing.

Whether or not the battle had been fought, the Russians would have been forced to surrender Moscow.

Whether or not the battle had been fought, the vast majority of Napoleon's *Grande Armée* would have died in the Russian winter as it withdrew westwards.

If anything at all was changed, it was that more of Napoleon's troops would have lived long enough to die during the retreat.

My thanks for help in writing this book go to Marcus Gaertner, who allowed me full access to his considerable collection and made several very useful suggestions as to which sources to consult, and to The Polish Institute Sikorsky Museum in London, which was as supportive as ever. Thanks are also due to Nikolai Ilyich and Timofei Nikolaiyevich Shevyakov (of the Moscow Grenadier Re-enactment Society) who spent so much time showing me around the battlefield in 1992 and 1993.

A word to the various spellings of Russian names. The source documents provide the following variations: Platow, Platov, Platof, and Platoff; Alsufev, Alsufiev, Alsufjef, Alsufjeff, Alsuvief; Uwarow, Uvarov, Uvarof, etc. This book has attempted to be consistent with the usage in Christopher Duffy's *Borodino: and the War of 1812*.

The extracts from *War and Peace* by L. N. Tolstoy, translated by Rosemary Edmonds (Penguin Classics 1957) © Rosemary Edmonds 1957, 1978 are reproduced by permission of Penguin Books Limited.

Digby Smith
Hanau, 1998.

FRENCH   RUSSIAN

HQ

Infantry

Cavalry

Artillery

Artillery deployed

Direction
of fire   uuuuuu   battery or more
                              ιｌｉ   less than a battery

Unit sizes

battalion   regiment   brigade

division   corps   army

N Napoleon   K Kutuzov

group of units
under one command

Movement

——————————→   Advance
— — — — — →   Withdrawal, French
- - - - - - →   Withdrawal, Russian

Defensive work   Jaegers

Defensive work   Bridge destroyed

Militia position   Watermill

Tactical Map Symbols

1

Introduction: Napoleon's Rise to Power and the Causes of the War of 1812

SINCE 1789, POLITICAL, MILITARY, and social development in Europe had been largely dictated by the dramatic — and often violent — events of the French revolution. France, one of the largest and most powerful nations in Europe, and indeed the world, was plunged into a period of chaotic change, civil war, and social upheaval.

Following the arrest of France's King Louis XVI in 1791, and the threats by the French revolutionary leaders to export their new political system to other European states, the monarchs in neighbouring countries joined together to form the First Coalition to destroy this virulent threat to their own crowned heads.

Louis was executed on the guillotine on 21 January 1793 and, until the Peace of Amiens (signed by France, Britain, Spain, and the Batavian Republic on 27 March 1802), revolutionary France fought the other major and minor European powers to a standstill on mainland Europe while losing most of her colonies to Britain, the now predominant global naval power.

During this turbulent period, one figure had risen to pre-eminence in France, Napoleon Bonaparte. Born in Ajaccio, Corsica, on 15 August 1769 — and of the Tuscan nobility — Napoleon studied at the military academy in Brienne from 1779 to 1784, and thence at the military college in Paris in 1785. Later that year, he was commissioned into the artillery. During the early revolutionary years, he was politically active with the Jacobins, and in 1791 he was elected lieutenant-colonel in the Ajaccio national guard. In 1793, he gained command of the artillery of the army besieging the allies in the major French naval base in Toulon, and used his guns to such good effect that they abandoned the place on 18 December of that year. On 22 December, Napoleon was promoted to général de brigade. During the popular unrest in Paris in October 1795, his 'whiff of grapeshot' saved the Convention which, in gratitude, promoted him to général de division. It is recorded that 200 of the mob were killed in this, Napoleon's next step up the ladder of success.

In 1796, Napoleon, with the Army of Italy, drove the Austrians out of northern Italy; in February 1797, he invaded Austria itself and secured the Peace of Campo Formio. Although France had beaten her mainland opposition (temporarily) into sullen submission, Britain, her most implacable foe, continued to defy her, protected by the dominating force of the Royal Navy. At Napoleon's suggestion, the Directory agreed to give him an army with which to seize Egypt and thus to threaten Britain's East Indian colonies. It was also a way for the Directory to be rid of an uncomfortably active and increasingly ambitious general.

On 1 July 1798, Napoleon and his army landed in Aboukir Bay to begin the conquest of Egypt, and at first all went in their favour; a month later, however, Admiral Horatio Nelson (who had been chasing this quarry for weeks) destroyed the French fleet at anchor in the Bay, and Napoleon and his army were marooned in Egypt. Napoleon's transport vessels were still intact, however, (but bottled up) in the harbour at Alexandria. Nothing daunted, Napoleon invaded Syria in February 1799 and laid siege to Acre on 17 March; a spirited defence – supported by Sir Sidney Smith and the Royal Navy – thwarted his aim and he was forced to raise the siege on 20 May, and to withdraw into Egypt with heavy losses. This was one of Napoleon's very rare defeats in the field. After languishing in Egypt for some months, Napoleon received news that political events in France were becoming volatile. Handing over command of his army to General Kleber, he took passage to France and was back in Paris in October 1799; his coup of 9 November of that year saw him installed as First Consul.

War broke out again and, in his victorious Marengo campaign in 1800, Napoleon drove the Austrians out of northern Italy, securing an advantageous peace for France at Luneville in February 1801. Relative peace followed and, in May 1802, Napoleon was declared First Consul for life by a grateful nation. On 18 May 1804, having discarded the now threadbare Jacobin costume which had served him so well so far, Napoleon crowned himself Emperor of the French. By 1805, however, Austria again took the field against France, only to be outwitted and humiliated by Napoleon in his famous Ulm campaign. With excruciat-ingly bad timing, Tsar Alexander I now sent an army under Field Marshal Kutuzov to aid the Austrians and was himself present at the 'Battle of the Three Emperors' at Austerlitz on 2 December 1805. With their armies crushed, the Tsar and Kaiser Franz II had no alternative but to sue for a humiliating peace (that of Pressburg, 26 December 1805) after which Napoleon formed the Confederation of the Rhine, a *cordon sanitaire* of minor German vassal states, made up largely of territories torn away from Austria at Pressburg.

In 1806, the weak King Frederick William III of Prussia bungled his decision-making process and declared war on France. The result was the lightning campaign of that autumn in which the much-vaunted Prussian army was largely destroyed in the twin battles of Jena and Auerstaedt on 14 October, and the string of shameful capitulations which followed them. In the Prussian capital city, Berlin, Napoleon dictated his famous Berlin Decrees, aimed at cutting off Britain from the European markets for her colonial products and manufactured goods. Increased sales of French colonial produce to the hungry Europeans were to fill the market vacuum thus created.

Tsar Alexander I had not learned the lesson of Austerlitz. He now sent an army under the incompetent General of Cavalry, Baron von Bennigsen, to co-operate with General L'Estocq's 20,000-strong corps which represented the remaining rump of the Prussian army. This coalition was finally defeated at the battle of Friedland on 14 June 1807. In the subsequent Treaty of Tilsit, signed by Napoleon, Alexander, and Frederick William III on a raft moored in the River Niemen on 9 July, Napoleon tightened his grip on mainland Europe, bringing Russia (at least temporarily) into his 'Continental System' of trade embargo against Britain.

It was in 1807 that Napoleon's meddlings in Spanish politics, and his occupation of Portugal following her refusal to adhere to his Berlin Decrees, lit the fuse of a patriotic fire in the Iberian peninsula which was to give Britain the long-sought-after opportunity to land an army, unopposed, on a friendly part of mainland Europe, remote from France, capable of being sustained by the Royal Navy and supported by the governments and armies (however ineffectively) of the area. This 'Spanish ulcer', as Napoleon termed it, was to tie down French (and allied) armies of up to 300,000 men and to cause them crippling casualties right through 1813.

Britain still held control of the world's oceans and schemed ceaselessly to bring Napoleon down. Her next attempt involved urging Austria to take the field again in 1809 with their hastily refurbished army together with its newly formed 'Landwehr', or territorial defence forces. Acting with his usual speed and energy, Napoleon thrust eastwards into Austria and was soon master of Vienna again, as he had been in 1805. This time, however, things were different, at least initially. Instead of suing at once for peace to regain his capital city, his opponent, Archduke Charles, offered battle when the French attempted to cross the River Danube on 21 and 22 May, and inflicted a smart defeat upon them at Aspern-Essling. Napoleon did not take this setback lying down; calling up his satellite army under Prince Eugène from northern Italy, he struck again, at Wagram, on 5 and 6 July, defeating the Austrians once more. In the following Peace of Schönbrunn on 10 October, Austria lost to Bavaria the provinces of Salzburg, Berchtesgaden, and the Inn-Hausrueck area;

Friaul, Trieste, Villach and those parts of Croatia and Dalmatia on the right bank of the River Save went to Napoleon; West Galicia and Krakau to the newly formed Grand Duchy of Warsaw, and part of East Galicia to Russia. This last was a reward for the services of a corps of 30,000 Russian troops in the conflict; the lack of aggression in their performance in this campaign did not escape Napoleon's notice, hence the relatively small size of Tsar Alexander's reward.

The Tsar was unhappy at the re-establishment of a Polish political entity (Warsaw) on his western border, despite it being – nominally at least – under the rule of the King of Saxony. This was because his western provinces were, in fact, old Polish lands which Russia had recently acquired during the various partitions of the defunct Kingdom of Poland among Prussia, Austria, and Russia in the 1790s. Much of the population of these provinces was still hostile to Russian rule. Caulaincourt, French ambassador to Russia, signed the Treaty of St Petersburg on 5 January 1810 with Alexander stating that the Kingdom of Poland would not be resurrected, but Napoleon refused to ratify the document, saying 'One cannot guarantee the future'.

Anxious to forge strategic alliances – and unsatisfied with the fidelity of his empress, Josephine – Napoleon divorced Josephine on 16 December 1809 and launched a request to Tsar Alexander for the hand of his younger sister, Anna. This request caused a horrified silence in St Petersburg but, while the Tsar stalled diplomatically, Napoleon sent a parallel request to the Emperor Franz of Austria, and on 2 April 1810, he married Grand Duchess Maria-Louise. The obvious affront to Alexander's family (regardless of the relief it also brought) did not go unnoticed.

In 1810, despite the 'Spanish ulcer', Napoleon was at the height of his power, but his ruthless and restless ambition recognised neither bounds nor satisfaction. While continuing an empty debate with the Tsar about the significance and future of the Grand Duchy of Warsaw, he planned, plotted, and tinkered incessantly with the map of Europe. He added the rump of the Electorate of Hanover to the recently created Kingdom of Westphalia; on 16 February he created the Grand Duchy of Frankfurt; on 9 July he annexed the Kingdom of Holland into France; on 12 November the Swiss Canton of Valais became the French *Département du Simplon*; and on 13 December, not satisfied that his Berlin Decrees and Continental System were being adequately enforced by his satraps, he simply annexed the Hanseatic towns of Hamburg, Bremen, and Lübeck, the Duchy of Lauenburg, and all the German coastal states from the River Ems to the River Elbe into France. This last, apparently simple, trick was to cost him dear although he did not yet realise it.

Among the territories that he had just devoured was one that was to give him a long-drawn-out, and ultimately fatal, bout of political indigestion – the Duchy of Oldenburg.

The poison pill contained in this seemingly innocuous morsel was the fact that the Duke (Friedrich August) was uncle to the Tsar, and both were members of the house of Holstein-Gottorp. Furthermore, the son of the Duke was married to the Tsar's sister. On being told of this, Napoleon informed the Duke that he might accept appropriate alternative estates or stay on in Oldenburg as he wished. The Duke decided to stay. When the Imperial French officials arrived in Oldenburg a few weeks later, however, they confiscated all moneys and told the Duke to resettle himself in Erfurt. As Erfurt was only about one-fifth the size of Oldenburg, the Duke was extremely unimpressed and cranked the Tsar into the equation. Alexander at once protested that the status of Oldenburg was guaranteed in Article 12 of the Treaty of Tilsit; secondly, if the duchy should become vacant, it was to revert to Russia; furthermore, Erfurt was totally inadequate as compensation for the dispossessed Duke.

The French foreign minister, de Champagny, at once generated volumes of obscure, meaningless diplomatic correspondence aimed at stalling any real progress in the matter, but the political situation began to fester. Meanwhile, the economies of mainland Europe were grinding to a halt under Napoleon's Continental System; widespread evasion of the System's regulations permitted extensive smuggling of banned British goods, and one of the most flagrant offenders was the Tsar's Russia. Napoleon was well informed of all of this and began to exert counter-pressure on Alexander to win greater leverage in the Oldenburg affair. At the same time, he had already realised that a break with Russia was inevitable and began to lay his plans for the invasion and subjugation of that gigantic country. Like his later counterparts, Adolf Hitler, Lenin, Stalin, and Saddam Hussein, he had already lost sight of the borderline between what was achievable and what was not.

There quickly developed an imperial (but diplomatically couched) slanging match. Napoleon took offence at Russia's occupation of Moldavia and Walachia (which occurred – without his blessing – in the aftermath of 1809), while the row over Russia's non-implementation of Napoleon's 'Decree of Trianon' of August 1810, specifically aimed to force the Tsar to stop his trade with Britain, was stepped up. The Tsar responded evasively, claiming that what happened in Russia were 'our private affairs . . . but we have confiscated 96 British ships'. Russia then complained that French colonial goods (from Ile-de-France, Batavia, and other locations) were flooding through France and into other European countries at inflated prices. Napoleon's reaction was to place import duties on tea, potash, and other Russian goods coming into his empire. In December 1810, the Tsar imposed high duties on imported French luxury goods; Napoleon's 'tit' for this 'tat' was to forbid the further importation of naval stores from Russia. The only effect of this brainwave was to line the pockets of many astute German merchants who became middlemen overnight and sold the same Russian goods on to the French Admiralty at inflated prices.

Meanwhile, the industrious Napoleon was forging political alliances for the coming war. To ex-marshal Bernadotte (now Crown Prince of Sweden) he wrote offering to restore Finland to Sweden (it had been taken by Russia in 1809) and to throw in Kurland and Livonia if Bernadotte would furnish him with a corps of 20,000 men for use against Russia. Bernadotte was not enthusiastic. Napoleon also considered that Caulaincourt, his ambassador to the Tsar in St Petersburg, had become contaminated with pro-Russian sentiment and replaced him with General Lauriston. On the military front, meanwhile, Napoleon's war machinery was grinding ahead at top speed. He ordered his planners to stockpile maps of eastern Europe and Russia; the arsenals produced weapons and equipment for the largest army that Europe had yet seen; artillery parks were moved from Ulm and Augsburg north-east to the Prussian fortresses of Küstrin, Glogau, Stettin, and to the free city of Danzig; the defences and garrisons of these places were strengthened; 80,000 French conscripts were called up in December 1810, and his planning staffs worked furiously to translate his ambitions into reality. These gargantuan preparations continued throughout 1811.

In July 1811, Frederick William III of Prussia sent General Scharnhorst to St Petersburg to negotiate a defensive pact and to proffer Prussian mediation with France on the Oldenburg problem; both offers were rejected.

Later, on 15 December 1811, Napoleon sent orders to his brother, Joseph (then King of Spain), that all cavalry and horse artillery of the Imperial Guard which were in that country were to be withdrawn from the Army of the North and sent back to France to refit and be brought up to strength. On 14 January 1812, he further ordered that all twenty-two battalions of infantry of the Young Guard (14,000 men of the divisions of Roguet and Dumoustier), and all Polish troops (1st–4th Infantry Regiments of the Vistula Legion, 4th, 7th, and 9th Infantry Regiments of the Grand Duchy of Warsaw, and the 7th, 8th, and 9th Polish Lancers) were also to leave Spain and march north. By this means, he withdrew 27,000 veteran troops from Spain to join his planned strike; but this still left 232,500 Imperial and allied soldiers there struggling, with diminishing success, to hold the lid on the increasingly adverse situation.

April and May 1812 saw further significant developments. On 5 April, Sweden and Russia signed a defensive pact by which Sweden was to receive Norway as a reward for supporting Russia against Napoleon. Tiring of Bernadotte's intransigence, Napoleon occupied his northern German province of Swedish Pomerania and the island of Rügen. In the south, Russia and Turkey signed the Peace of Bucharest on 28 May, thus releasing Admiral Chichagov to march north with 25,000 men to join in opposing the Corsican's threatening invasion.

Napoleon, of course, had long been stirring up trouble between Russia and Turkey, and, when Kutuzov forced the Turks into an armistice and peace negotiations after surrounding their army at Slobodzia on 4 July 1811, he burst out : *'conçoit-on ces chiens, ces gredins de Turcs, qui on eu le talent de se faire battre de la sorte! Qui est-ce qui aurait pu le prévoir?'* [How can one comprehend these dogs, these scoundrels of Turks who have such a talent to get themselves beaten in this way! Who could have foreseen this?]. There were many in France (the growing anti-war party) who hoped that this blow would have been enough to cause Napoleon to call off his invasion plans.

On 24 February 1812, France and Prussia signed an offensive–defensive alliance; Prussia was to provide a corps of 20,000 men and sixty guns for use as Napoleon's northern flank guard in Russia and to strengthen the garrisons in Colberg, Potsdam, Graudenz, and the Silesian fortresses. In return, Napoleon would enlarge Prussia once he had dealt with Alexander. From his father-in-law Napoleon cajoled an Austrian corps of 23,500 infantry, 4500 cavalry, 2000 artillery, and ninety guns under General-of-Cavalry, Prince Schwarzenberg, to act as his southern flank guard on his advance into Russia. As his armies began to form up along Russia's western border, Napoleon continued his diplomatic dialogue with the Tsar.

On 25 February he spoke with General Chernyshev – an aide-de-camp (ADC) to Alexander – offering to stop his war preparations on the following terms:

1 Exact application by Russia of the embargo on English goods.
2 Negotiation of a new Franco-Russian trade agreement.
3 Solution of the Oldenburg problem (but neither Danzig nor Warsaw could be part of the duke's compensation).

Alexander replied agreeing in principle but adding that the garrison of Danzig must be greatly reduced and that French troops must evacuate Prussia. To Napoleon, of course, this reply amounted to 'an insult' as he told Prince Kurakin, Alexander's ambassador.

The next move was for Napoleon to send Count Narbonne to St

Petersburg with a lengthy letter to the Tsar; Narbonne's real aim was to spy. Judging the diplomatic possibilities now to have been exhausted, Kurakin requested his passport from the French Foreign Minister on 7 May, but the Duke of Bassano ignored his request and left Paris to go to Dresden for the forthcoming gathering of Napoleon's allies in that city. On 9 May, Napoleon left St Cloud and set off on his epic adventure towards Russia. He reached Dresden on 16 May. Next day, Kaiser Franz of Austria and all the princes of the Confederation of the Rhine arrived there and, on 26 May, King Frederick William III of Prussia completed the party.

Count Narbonne, meanwhile, had reached Alexander's court at Vilnius at the end of April, having made a detour to that city via St Petersburg. Alexander had decided to take personal command of his armies and had moved out of his summer capital to set up his headquarters in Vilnius, close to Russia's western borders. It was also the headquarters of the 1st Russian Army of the West. Narbonne's presence was tolerated, but he saw very little of any significance and achieved nothing. Meanwhile, the storm continued to gather at increasing speed. Napoleon was in Danzig from 7 to 12 June, during which time he declared: 'Danzig is French'. He then moved on north-eastwards to Königsberg, left again on 16 June, and went further east via Insterburg (now Chernyakhovsk) and Gumbinnen (now Gusev) to Wilkowischki, on the road towards Vilnius.

The storm was about to break and the Russians were pitifully ill-prepared to weather it.

THE BALANCE OF FORCES

Napoleon had gathered together an army of truly astounding size and composition. Estimates vary as to exactly how many men crossed the Russian border in June 1812, but the following table shows (on the left) the *Grande Armée*'s strength as at the crossing of the River Niemen on 23 June. Russian forces are shown on the right.

As can clearly be seen, the Russians were initially outnumbered in every sector of the front. As the French advanced further into the country, however, the frightening wastage that they suffered (particularly in cavalry horses) coupled with their combat losses, began to even the scales. Even so, it was only on the southern flank in September, that Chichagov's arrival with his army from the Turkish frontier gave them superiority of numbers anywhere.

The national composition of Napoleon's army is also of interest:

French and Allies			Russian		
	men	guns	men	guns	
		in Latvia			
X Corps	28,100	100	14,000	54	Army of Finland
			12,000	24	Essen's Corps
Total	28,100	100	26,000	78	*Total* (as of 23 Sept.)
		at Polotzk			
II Corps	40,000	114			
VI Corps	36,000	50	21,850	96	I Corps
Total	76,000	164	21,850	96	*Total*
		on the North-central Front			
Napoleon's Main Body			*Barclay's 1st Army of the West*		
Imperial Guard	51,328	150	16,860	84	II Corps
I Corps	70,000	240	17,850	84	III Corps
III Corps	37,889	90	15,200	72	IV Corps
IV Corps	49,850	100	20,120	80	V Corps
I Cavalry Corps	10,795	24	16,860	84	VI Corps
II Cavalry Corps	10,974	24	3,700	12	I Cavalry Corps
			3,580	12	II Cavalry Corps
			3,020	12	III Cavalry Corps
			6,380	12	Cossacks
			720	36	Artillery Reserve
Total	230,836	628	104,290	488	*Total*
		Later Reinforcements			
IX Corps	33,500	70			
(at Vilnius on 7 September)					
XI Corps	14,000	48			
(at Vilnius on 22 November)					
Total	47,500	118			
		the South-central Front			
King Jérôme's Group			*Bagration's 2nd Army of the West*		
V Corps	36,000	140	17,110	84	VII Corps
VIII Corps	22,974	44	15,840	60	VIII Corps
III Cavalry Corps	9,081	24	3,580	12	IV Cavalry Corps
IV Cavalry Corps	7,100	24	4,180	12	Cossacks
			7,200	12	27th Division
Total	75,155	232	47,910	180	*Total*
		on the South Flank			
Prince Schwarzenberg's Group			*Tormasov's 3rd Army of the West*		
VII Corps	19,313	40	11,870	46	Kamenski's Corps
The Austrian Corps	30,000	90	16,860	82	Markov's Corps
			5,940	24	Sacken's Reserve
			6,040		Lambert's Corps
			3,960		Irregulars
			240	12	Artillery Reserve
Total	49,313	130	44,910	164	*Total*
			Chichagov's Army of the Danube		
			(arrived in early September)		
			8,700	48	I Corps
			8,700	48	II Corps
			8,700	48	III Corps
			6,500	48	IV Corps
			6,000	12	Lüder's Corps
			38,600	204	*Total*

Nationality	Battalions	Squadrons	Batteries	Men
French and 'new French'*	239	214	76	212,666
Poles (and Lithuanians)	51	69	9	74,700
Austrians	32	50	14	30,904
Bavarians	30	24	8	30,100
Saxons	22	32	6	19,980
Westphalians	22	20	6	27,832
Prussians	20	24	7½	20,000
Italians	22	14	10	15,597
Neapolitans	16	8	3	11,800
Württembergers	12	16	6	15,800
Swiss	12			6,073
German mini-states**	11			7,195
Grand Duchy of Berg	8	4	2	5,000
Grand Duchy of Baden	5	4	1	7,666
Grand Duchy of Hessen-Darmstadt	6	3	1	5,000
Croats, Illyrians, and Dalmatians	10			7,446
Portuguese	6	3		3,958
Spanish	4			3,054
Würzburg	3			2,400
Mecklenburgers	3			2,218
Mamelukes		½		75
Total	534	485½	149½	509,464

* = Dutch, Belgian, Hanseatics, Lauenburg, Oldenburg etc.
** = Frankfurt, Saxon Duchies, Thüringian states, Lippe

THE OPPOSING PLANS

The French plan

Napoleon's plan (at least the initial phase) was simple and, in principle, a repetition of his German campaigns of 1805, 1806, and 1809. Keeping the enemy in ignorance of his exact aims, locations, and strengths, he would concentrate in overwhelming superiority at a chosen point, rush at the unsuspecting foe, destroy the major part of the enemy's field forces, and dictate peace on his own terms. Fully aware of the vast scope of Russia, he did not plan to advance too far eastwards and certainly had no intention (at this point) of marching to Moscow in 1812. His intelligence network had given him a fairly clear picture of the Russian strengths and dispositions, and he had every confidence that he could achieve his desired victory within a few weeks.

Basically, the plan was as follows: while the north and south flank guards advanced to protect his vulnerable lines of supply and communication, Napoleon's main central group (including Oudinot's II Corps) was to smash Barclay de Tolly's 1st Army, which was concentrated around Vilnius. To his south, the group commanded by his brother, King Jérôme of Westphalia (V, VII, VIII, Infantry and IV Cavalry Corps) was to encircle and destroy Bagration's 2nd Army, which was situated east of Bialystok and well separated from Bagration in distance [about 40 miles (60 km)] and by the obstacle of the upper Niemen. To exploit this potentially fatal gap in the Russian front, Marshal Davout's I Corps was to advance rapidly eastwards to seize the town of Minsk thus blocking any attempt by Alexander to unite his 1st and 2nd Armies in western Russia.

With his well-practised staff, working under the faithful and indefatigable Alexander Berthier, having the initiative and the element of surprise firmly in his grasp, and with experienced and successful commanders at all levels of his vast army, there seemed to be no reason in the world for this plan not to bring the early victory that he had calculated upon. But fail it did.

For some reason, the position of Jérôme's group [spread out from Warsaw in the north-west to the area of the River Bug – 100 miles (160 km) to the south-east – to facilitate foraging prior to advancing eastwards] was wrongly assessed in relation to the speed of the 'lunge' that they would have to make to catch and destroy Bagration's 2nd Army. As General Ochs's biographer, Leopold, Freiherr von Holzhausen, recorded:

On 14 June the king [Jérôme] received orders to cross the River Niemen at Grodno. As the right wing of the *Grande Armée* had previously been designated to operate against Volyniya [the present-day Ukraine], most of the troops were located in this direction and needed several marches to reach their new line of operations.

By 17/18 June the Westphalian Corps was concentrated around Pultusk [30 miles (50 km) north of Warsaw] and set off by forced marches behind V (Polish) Corps via Ostrolenka [on the River Narew], Szczuczyn and Augustów towards Grodno. [From Pultusk to Grodno was a distance of about 155 miles (250 km); marching at a rate of 12 miles (20 km) per day – as in the Nijmegen Marches – this would take about twelve days on good roads with healthy, well-nourished men. In Lithuania in 1812, none of these criteria applied.]

Napoleon and the main body of the army crossed the River Niemen at Kovno on 23/24 June and the advanced guard entered Vilnius 28 June. Napoleon's aim was to prevent the unification of the 1st and 2nd Russian Armies . . . this gave the king of Westphalia the task of catching up with Bagration's 2nd Army and bringing him to battle while Davout, with 40,000 men, raced for Minsk, to turn Bagration's northern flank and cut him off from Barclay de Tolly's 1st Army.

Jérôme tried to fulfil the Emperor's wishes by pushing on at full speed with more forced marches but, despite all the efforts of his men, his advanced guard reached Grodno only on 28 June. The Russians had

The Balance of Forces in 1812

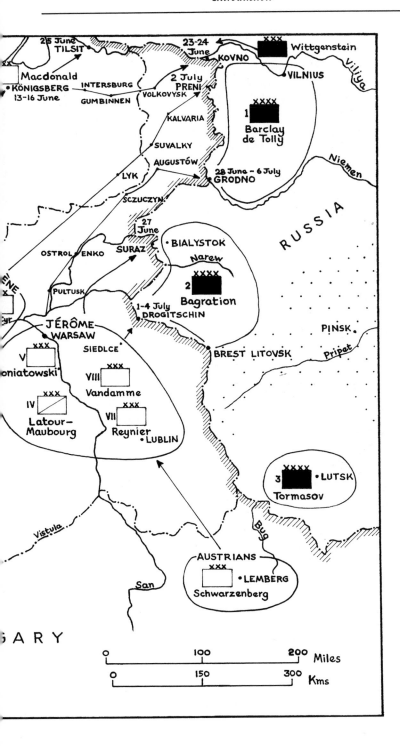

broken the bridges; General Allix had them rapidly rebuilt, and the VIII Corps entered Grodno that same day. There was a minor brush with some of Platov's Cossacks who lost about 100 men.

King Jérôme entered the town with his guard cavalry and a Polish division on 28 June; the Westphalian infantry [those that had not fallen out with exhaustion or died of fatigue] came in on 2 July.

Napoleon made Jérôme entirely responsible for Bagration's escape, forgetting that on 14 June his V and VIII Corps were still in cantonments on the Vistula and the Bug. Jérôme now allowed his shattered troops two days' rest so that the stragglers could catch up.

But this failure in the southern sector of the central front (which resulted in a furious Napoleon sacking his unfortunate brother) was not the only thing that went wrong in this Great Plan. Napoleon's personally led main group to the north of Jérôme's was also unable to bring its prey (Barclay) to battle when it rushed across the Niemen on 23 and 24 June 1812, and both main Russian armies escaped intact to the east to fight another day. True, their initial attempts to join up were frustrated at Mir on 10 July and at Saltanovka (Mogilev) on 23 July, but their critically important junction took place at Smolensk on 1 August.

If Jérôme was late at Grodno on 28 June, Prince Eugène's central group (IV and VI Corps and III Cavalry Corps) was even further behind. They reached the Niemen at the village of Preni [about 19 miles (30 km) south of Kovno] only on 2 July, Novi Troki on 12 July, and were reviewed by Napoleon at Vilnius two days later.

The cost of the pursuit had been high, (and would continue to be so) despite the almost total lack of contact with the enemy, as can be seen from the parade states shown below:

Corps	23 June	20 July	28 July
V (Poles)	30,000	23,000	22,000
VII (Saxons)	17,000	14,000	13,000
VIII (Westphalians)	18,000	14,000	10,000
IV Cavalry Corps	10,000	6,500	5,000
Totals	75,000	57,500	50,000
Deficit		17,500	25,000

In other words, four weeks after the start of operations, this force had lost one-third of its effective soldiers and had been involved in only relatively minor skirmishes!

Colonel Thomasset, commanding officer of the 3rd Swiss Infantry Regiment (9th Division, II Corps), described the terrible conditions of this initial advance to contact in a letter to Colonel von May at the regimental depot in Lille on 10 July:

You can have no concept of what we have suffered in this campaign. We have not had any bread for two months; only a little flour of which each soldier carries four pounds in a small sack. The entire country is devastated, the houses are looted, the peasants have fled. We have lost an incredible number of men due to the forced marches that we have had to make. We had to march 12 *Meilen* [1 Meil = 4.7 miles (7.5 km)] in 24 hours which drove our agony to the limit and meant that two-thirds of the men fell out and are now with the stragglers. They are trickling back day by day; I have met many, particularly from the 3rd Regiment . . . The wagons are always behind owing to lack of horses; we replace them with whatever we can find, but the regiment loses about twenty per day despite this. The [regimental] artillery is without teams; the regiment now has no more than ten of the horses that we bought in Nijmegen. There have been two skirmishes with the enemy in the advance so far, one east of Vilnius, one at Vilkomir; we had to deploy only two infantry regiments to put to flight a corps of 25,000 men. There are rumours of an early peace; I hope they are true and that we can leave this terrible land. The war in Spain was child's play (*une plaisanterie*) compared to this, where we are short of everything; I haven't drunk any wine for two months.

Another Swiss, Captain Rosselet, added his contribution to the record of this desperate period: 'By day great heat; terrible storms with thunder and hail; by night, floods and cold in our wet clothes. It's terrible to bivouac in these conditions. Many have dysentery.' After several days of terrible heat, a gigantic thunderstorm burst over the weary columns as they struggled forward, bringing five days of torrential rain and a sudden, sharp – and unpleasant – drop in the temperature. The 'roads' and fields were flooded; all movement of the lumbering wagons stopped as their teams of starved, exhausted draught animals collapsed and died in the mud. The already bad supply situation for the troops became catastrophic; the bivouacs in the fields of half-grown barley became swamps. The problem of stragglers was already serious and quickly became acute and chronic as thousands left their regiments to forage on their own account: many never to return to their colours; many to die at the hands of the enraged Russian peasants.

The war in Russia was quickly assuming the same characteristics as that in Spain: a struggle of the entire population against the invaders.

Russia was saved, although much blood and sacrifice yet lay ahead. Let us now examine the Russian plans to establish how far they contributed to this – for Napoleon – so fateful a development.

The Russian plans

'If I were to be supreme army commander in a war against Napoleon, I would avoid a major battle and withdraw for so long that the French, instead of winning a great victory, would suffer a second Poltava.'

These unwittingly prophetic words, with their reference to the crushing defeat of King Charles XII of Sweden by Peter the Great on 8 July 1709, were spoken by General Barclay de Tolly in 1807 as he was recovering in hospital from wounds after the battle of Prüssisch-Eylau. By early 1812, however, Barclay's strategic vision had lost its clarity to such an extent that he was unable to convince the Tsar, or his peers, of the need to adopt this course of action, even though he was by then Minister for War.

In contrast to Napoleon's headquarters, where everything was decided and executed in accordance with his clearly defined, relentlessly logical strategic plans, Alexander's headquarters in Vilnius in early 1812 was a tower of babel, confused with conflicting plans and awash with indiscipline, indecision, and intrigue. Blame for this situation must rest with the Tsar but, to his credit, he eventually realised his own shortcomings before irreparable harm was done, and he left the army's headquarters on 18 July to return to Moscow to organise the national war effort.

This chaotic situation had grown up 'like topsy' over a period of five years as follows.

After Prussia's crushing defeats in 1806 and 1807, many senior officers left this service and took positions in foreign armies, several of them entering Russian service. Here, together with other foreign *émigrés*, they were generously received by the Tsar and frequently installed in comfortable, influential sinecures close to the throne, where they often displaced capable Russian officers. Many of them never even bothered to learn the language of their adoptive home, and this helped to increase the atmosphere of mistrust and mutual hostility which, by 1812, had become endemic in Russian army headquarters. Of the various plans considered by Alexander and his staff, those below were the main contenders.

1   General Volzogen had heard of Barclay's ideas on a possible defence against a French invasion; using these as a basis, he drew up his own plan and sent it to Prince Volkonsky, Quartermaster-General of the Russian army, as early as August 1810. Among other things, he stated that:

> the fortresses along Russia's western border will offer no defence against Napoleon. The protection of an area can be secured only by the destruction of the enemy army, even if this means withdrawing hundreds of miles into the interior. Thus we should select and build a few very strong, well-stocked fortresses well back from the western frontier, supported by fortified depots and a strong operational army to block the

enemy advance. A second strong field army should also be formed to operate against the enemy's lines of communication.

2   The French *émigré* Count d'Allonville submitted a paper (*'Mémoire politique et militaire sur les circonstances presentes'*) to the Tsar's headquarters in January 1811. It included political as well as military advice:

> . . . form alliances . . . take pre-emptive strikes against Warsaw and Silesia together with Prussian troops. If forced to withdraw, destroy the assets in Warsaw and Silesia before you leave and fall back on Moscow. . . . Fortify the lines of the Rivers Oder, Vistula, and Dnieper . . . send Cossacks to harry the enemy flanks and rear. Form two reserve armies at Kiev and Smolensk . . . operate offensively whenever possible. d'Allonville calculated the troops needed for this strategy as follows: the operational army – 80–100,000 men; a corps on the Austrian frontier – 30–40,000 men; a corps to support the Prussian army – 20–30,000 men; the two reserve armies at Smolensk and Kiev – 40–50,000 men each; a diversionary expedition to Naples – 10,000 men; another 10,000 against southern France [both these last to be undertaken in co-operation with British naval and military assistance]; 20–30,000 men to be deployed as garrisons and raiding columns. Total manpower required – 250–325,000 men.

This plan was delivered to Alexander by Admiral Mordvinov in January 1812 together with two other documents: a study of Peter the Great's withdrawal before Charles XII and a paper on the Duke of Wellington's withdrawal into the lines of Torres Vedras. It is not known how much impact the plan had on the Tsar, but he did not pursue the suggestion of allying himself with Prussia. The projected diversionary raids on Naples and France were far too weak and too remote to have posed serious threats to any Napoleonic invasion of Russia, and would just have squandered valuable resources.

3   Count von Toll presented a plan to the Tsar through Prince Peter Volkonsky in Vilnius on 29 April 1812. It contained the following criticism:

> The present dispositions of the Russian army are not good because the two main armies are too far apart even though General Essen's Corps of Observation is linking them. They may be defeated in detail. . . . It is too late for us to advance into Warsaw; anyway, the French have already stripped it bare . . . the French have concentrated over 220,000 men and outnumber each of our armies. We must adopt a defensive posture . . . Count Wittgenstein's I Corps of 18,000 men should advance to Kovno to observe enemy activity, block any advance up the Niemen and cover Lithuania and Kurland. The 1st Army of the West should be concentrated more densely and to the west . . . The 2nd Army of the West should also concentrate to the west so as to be able to operate against the southern

flank of any enemy advance on Moscow . . . The troops of these two armies can only stay in these positions as long as the enemy stays in Warsaw. If the enemy advances eastward, they risk being defeated in detail. I suggest therefore, that rearward locations be pre-identified to which they should then fall back and concentrate. . . . our forces are currently stretched out from Brest Litovsk to Sukhovola, a distance of over 176 versts [1 verst = 0.66 mile (1.067 km)] which represents seventy hours forced march. . . The war with Turkey must be concluded as soon as possible so that the Army of the Danube may be moved north to support the 1st and 2nd Armies . . . The grain stored in Kurland should be moved east to Libau and Windau (leaving only sufficient stocks to maintain the local populace) and thence by river to Riga. The grain in Lithuania should be moved east to Kovno, Ponewiesch, Janow and Wilkomir. The grain stored in the magazines at Slonim and Pinsk should be tripled.

From the above, it is clear that von Toll was ignorant of the true strength of the *Grande Armée* when he prepared his plan.

4   General von Phull, an ex-staff officer of the Prussian army and personal 'guru' on military strategic matters to Alexander, also drew up a plan for the defence of Russia against Napoleon and it was his plan which was adopted, at least for the initial phase of the campaign. When its inherent defects became apparent, however, it was abandoned and the original 'Barclay Plan' of 1807 was followed, at least until Barclay was replaced by Kutuzov as commander-in-chief of the Russian armies and modified the plan to give battle at Borodino to avoid handing over Moscow to the invaders without a fight.

Before examining von Phull's plan, however, it will be rewarding to hear what the great Carl von Clausewitz, a contemporary of his, had to say about the man who held such sway over the Tsar.

I went to Vilnius (the headquarters of Barclay de Tolly and Tsar Alexander) in April 1812. Many other ex-Prussian officers were also there including Count Chasot, who was *en route* to take service in England as he did not speak Russian and did not want to hang around on Alexander's staff without a field command. He was very pessimistic about Russia's chances in the coming campaign, mainly as a result of his observations made in Alexander's headquarters. Chasot opined that the only hope for the Russians was that Napoleon would commit so many blunders that he would defeat himself. Cynics might say that in the end, it was the 'Chasot Plan' which indeed saved Russia.

Alexander, although never having served in the army, wanted to exercise supreme command himself. He felt qualified for this post on the basis of the years of private tuition which he had received in St Petersburg at Phull's hands. Phull had been an officer in the Prussian General Staff and left

Prussian service after the disasters of 1806 to take Russian service. He, Massenbach, and Scharnhorst were the three senior members of the Prussian General Staff during the campaign of 1806 and he was regarded by his contemporaries as somewhat of a genius. He was a great admirer of Julius Caesar and Frederick the Great but had no conception of modern warfare. He was a sworn enemy of common Philistines, superficiality, lies, and weaknesses; this gave him an air of great strength, depth and genius. I have never seen anyone lose his head more quickly, or anyone who, obsessed by a great strategic vision, be so put out by simple, everyday, real-world problems. He was extremely sensitive and could not stand any criticism of his theories; until 1812 he did not have to.

In the Revolutionary Wars he played only a minor part and only after the fighting ceased did he become General Quartermaster to Field Marshal Möllendorf. During the subsequent years of peace as a staff officer, he lived – as did the other staff officers – in a world of war games and imaginary actions. In 1806 he was a staff officer to King Frederick William III of Prussia but, as the king did not command, Phull did nothing. After the catastrophes of Jena and Auerstedt, his irony burst forth; he laughed like a maniac at the destruction of our army. Instead of coming forward to help fill the great spiritual vacuum which had settled on the Prussian state and army after the defeat, to prove his practical virtuosity as Scharnhorst did, he resigned and took Russian service. In Möllendorf's headquarters in Hochheim in 1795, Phull announced 'I'm not bothering with anything anymore because it's all going to the devil anyway!'

In 1806, while fleeing from the French, he took off his hat and cried 'Adieu, Prussian monarchy!' In November 1812, in St Petersburg, after the French had begun their retreat, he said to me 'Believe me, no good will come of this!' Phull had not changed one whit over the years; he did, however, have a true heart and a selfless character.

Phull had not troubled to learn Russian, had not acquainted himself with the leading members of the state or army and knew nothing of their organisation. Alexander decided to treat him as an abstract genius who could not be expected to carry out mundane, practical tasks.

Phull's plan was selected by the Tsar without reference to his Minister for War (Barclay) who disagreed with it – as many others also did – but had no choice but to try to put it into effect.

Clausewitz had no faith in the plan either and, indeed, its flaws were many, mainly because its author had developed it in splendid isolation in his ivory tower in Vilnius. The basic problem was that western Russia contained precious few natural obstacles of any strength, and even the major rivers were frequently fordable in many places. Extensive reconnaissances did locate a reasonably suitable site at Drissa on the River Duena, however, and von Phull decided to make this the central feature of his entire defensive strategy. The main problem was that Drissa was in the wrong place. From history, all knew that Napoleon's targets would be firstly to destroy the Russian field army and, if this failed, to occupy Russia's capital city to break their will to continue the struggle. Russia, of course, had two capitals; St Petersburg (in the summer) and Moscow (for the winter), and Drissa lay between the two approach routes to these targets, blocked neither, and was too remote from either to exercise any strategic influence on an invading army aimed at either city. Nevertheless, the place was surveyed, funds, materials, and manpower allocated, and much work done to build the planned fortifications.

> Phull calculated that the camp would need 130,000 men to defend it but in fact, the 1st Army (to whom this task would fall) could be brought up to only 100,000. Apart from inadequate forces, the fortified camp was constructed on the western side of the river (it was, in fact, a bridgehead), the river was fordable at several points both up- and downstream of it and no provision had been made to fortify the eastern bank or to ensure that adequate forces would be available to man these works if they were to be built.
>
> Phull also agreed with many others that the 2nd Army should operate alone against the southern flank of the invading army but this was a very dangerous proposal as it split the available forces and the 2nd Army was so weak that it could be held in check by a small enemy force, kept in isolation from the 1st Army and destroyed at will.
>
> No-one in the Vilnius headquarters knew what to do with the Drissa fortifications, but no-one could muster up enough courage to tell the Tsar that Phull's plan was irrelevant if not downright suicidal. Phull could not have done a better job for Napoleon if he had tried!
>
> The 'Drissa Plan' did have one redeeming feature: it called for the 1st Army to fall back into the camp if the enemy advanced and not to stand and fight in the forward defensive stance which it occupied at the start of the campaign. This fact probably saved the Russian army in 1812.

Clausewitz has also left us his observations on the make-up and working methods of Alexander's staff and of von Phull's role in it. By this time, Clausewitz (then a lieutenant-colonel) had been appointed aide-de-camp (ADC) to von Phull, a somewhat invidious position for him when he realised the gravity of the errors of the plan with which he had now become closely identified.

> Alexander's staff consisted of Prince Volkonsky (1st General Adjutant and Administrative Chief of the General Staff, who, however, failed to take over any active role in the planning or execution of operational matters);

General Count Arakcheev (a long-time confidant of the Tsar, a ferocious disciplinarian, greatly feared by many); General Arenfeldt (a Swede, ADC to the Tsar and an active intriguer); General Count Bennigsen (given no specific responsibilities owing to his poor performance in the campaign of 1807; he was merely a courtier, he had estates near Vilnius); General Barclay de Tolly (Minister for War, General officer Commanding the 1st Army, with the 2nd Army also under command).

Alexander held no regular staff meetings and Barclay usually issued the daily orders although Prince Volkonsky occasionally gave some as did Phull. Phull lived in complete isolation in imperial headquarters in Vilnius; he had no official position, no authority, no adjutants, no office; he received no reports, had no information as to the status or situation of the army (or of the enemy) and had absolutely no contact with Barclay.

Owing to Napoleon's good operational security, Alexander's staff had no real idea of the enemy's strength but assessed it as about 600,0000 men.

This pessimistic view of the Russian army was not shared by all, however. Prince Eugen of Württemberg (commander of the 4th Division of the Russian army through 1812) bears witness to the fact that the intrigue and political in-fighting in the imperial headquarters did not affect the morale or the combat quality of the officers and soldiers lower down the tree. He wrote:

Clausewitz is completely wrong when he states that the condition of the Russian army was poor or even desperate. He was possibly influenced by the differences of opinion in the headquarters. The spirit of the troops, and their discipline, remained immune from any negative effects of such quarrels. The rearguard always fought bravely and to advantage. We followed their fate with great interest; the regiments competed for the honour of taking part in these combats. Those who did not take part in such actions remained in good heart in their bivouacs. I can swear that this was how things were. Of course, there were some who insisted that the German, Barclay, and all foreigners who accompanied him were traitors. But this was discounted by all who knew the true state of affairs. At least this was so in my division. I refer the reader to Danilevsky, Volume I, pages 220, 221 and Volume II, pages 145 and 146 for the full justification of Barclay's services to the Russian Empire.

By 1 May 1812 the Russian army was in the process of being rapidly expanded and had reached the following status:

Guards infantry (6 regiments and 1 battalion) – 19 battalions; line infantry (164 regiments including Jaegers and naval battalions) – 492 battalions; 3 grenadier instruction battalions.
Total Infantry = 514 battalions

Guards cavalry (6 regiments and 2 Cossack sotnias) – 30 squadrons; 60 line cavalry regiments – 380 squadrons
Total Cavalry = 410 squadrons.

Guards artillery (4 foot and 2 horse batteries) – 6 batteries; the line – 27 field brigades (81 batteries),10 reserve brigades (40 batteries), 4 depot brigades (32 batteries)
Total Artillery = 159 batteries.

Pioniers – (2 regiments) 6 battalions.

Total under Arms – *c.* 480,000 men and 1600 guns.

Not all of these assets were available for use against Napoleon, however; the following must be subtracted:

The Army of the Danube (Kutuzov) on the Turkish frontier – 6th and 7th Cavalry Divisions, 8th, 9th, 10th, 15th, 16th, and 22nd Infantry Divisions: 87,000 men.

In the Crimea and New Russia (Duke Richelieu) – 8th Cavalry Division, 13th Infantry Division, and the eight depot battalions of the 9th Infantry Division: 19,500 men.

In the Caucasian Lines (General Rushchev): one dragoon regiment and four infantry regiments of the 19th Division, the Garrison Regiments Astrakhan, Kisljaer, Vladikavkas, and one battalion of the Garrison Regiment Mosdok: 17,000 men.

In Grusien (General Marquis Paulucci) – two dragoon regiments, 20th Infantry Division and the rest of the 19th Division: 24,000 men.

In Finland (General Steinheil) – two dragoon regiments, 6th, 21st, and 25th Infantry Divisions: 30,000 men.

In Moscow the newly forming 27th Infantry Division: 8000 men.

Instruction battalions, pionier battalions, and reserve artillery: 12,000 men.

Thus, in western Russia were about 280,000 men, including 80,000 depot troops. The depot troops were made up of the 2nd Battalions of each infantry regiment and the 5th, 9th, and 10th squadrons of each cavalry regiment but, of these, 12 battalions and 16 squadrons had been formed into a Reserve of 35,000 men who were deployed along the Rivers Dvina, Dnieper, and Beresina and at Mosir on the Pripet.

A Second Reserve was formed from recruit-training depots and was deployed in three lines as follows:

1st Line (19 battalions) in the towns of Steraja Russa, Toronez, Vyazma, Roslavl, Starodub, Konotop, and Olviopol.

2nd Line (9 battalions) in Petrozavodsk, Novgorod, Tver, Moscow, Kaluga, Orel, Kursk, Kharkov and Ekaterinoslav.

3rd Line (5 battalions) in Kargopol and Olonez for Finland, near Slavyenozerbsk for the 13th Division in Odessa and the Crimea and in Taganrog and Azov for the Caucasian Lines and Gruza.

New recruits were concentrated into 4th (Reserve) Battalions, each of three companies, for the line infantry regiments; 6th (Reserve) Squadrons for the cuirassier and dragoon regiments, and 11th and 12th Squadrons of the hussar and lancer regiments at 150 mounted men per squadron.

In March 1812 the 2nd (Depot) Battalions (less their two grenadier companies) and the 4th (Reserve) Battalions of the line infantry regiments were formed into eighteen new infantry divisions; eight new cavalry divisions and twenty-five new artillery batteries were raised in the same way.

Fifty-eight Artillery Depot Parks were organised into three 'lines'. 1st Line parks were fully mobile and stocked with powder, shot, shell, flints, and all necessary laboratory tools and equipment; 2nd and 3rd Line parks had no horses but resupplied the 1st Line parks with ammunition and other requisites by means of transport provided by the civil authorities.

An extensive system of ration and forage magazines had also been established: at Riga and Duenaburg were stockpiled supplies for eight infantry and four cavalry divisions each for one month; at Drissa were four days' rations; in Disna were thirteen days' rations and ten days' oats. Other depots were established as follows:

Location	Supplies for (weeks)	Infantry Divisions	Cavalry Divisions
Velikiye Luki	1	8	4
Novgorod	1	8	4
Bobruysk	4	2	1
Mogilev	8	2	1
Kiev	4	9	4
Sossniza	8	9	4★
Swenziany	4	8	4

★ = not complete

In Grodno, Brest, Slonim, Sluzk, Pinsk, and Mosir were each one month's supplies for two infantry and one cavalry divisions, and in Lutzk were two months' supplies for nine infantry and four cavalry divisions.

As events (and the adoption of von Phull's plan) proved, these magazines were too large and sited too far to the west, but most of them were eaten down before falling into enemy hands, or were burned. There were insufficient bakeries and, when requisitioning was introduced, it failed owing to the rapid enemy advance and the scarcity of local produce. The Russian army suffered much hardship during the retreat along the upper reaches of the River Dvina (after abandoning the Drissa camp) because their strategic plans had not foreseen operations in this area and no magazines had been established there. The difficulties that faced the *Grande Armée* during its advance, through a devastated countryside and with no effective supply system of its own, have been graphically recorded by many of the unfortunates who survived the campaign.

In August, the Tsar introduced a Grocery Tax on the populace in the area of operations; it was paid in black bread, barley, and oats, and worked very well after Borodino. During the pursuit of the beaten invaders in November, the supply situation of the Russians was helped immensely by their capture of Napoleon's great depot in Minsk, on 17 November, and of that in Vilnius on 8 December.

2

The Invasion

DIPLOMATIC DISCUSSION REGARDING the validity of von Phull's 'Drissa Plan' gradually gathered momentum in Vilnius, and, on 23 June (the day of the invasion!), Clausewitz was sent off by von Phull to Drissa to inspect the works and report on progress. Arriving there armed only with an order written in French by von Phull, he was at once taken for a French spy and had great difficulty convincing the local commander of his actual status. Eventually, he was allowed to conduct his survey, and found that a triple line of earthworks had been built, some open to the rear, others closed, but there were no palisades, *chevaux de frise*, wolf pits, or other obstacles. None of the planned seven bridges connecting the camp to the eastern bank had been built, and the officer in charge of this particular project had no idea of how to go about constructing them! Clausewitz assured him that he would have an officer of engineers sent to take over this work and left to return to Vilnius. He arrived at Swenziany (three days' march north-east of Vilnius) on 28 June to find Alexander's headquarters there; the enemy had crossed the Niemen the day he left, and the war was in full swing.

Despite the need for a speedy advance if Napoleon's plan to destroy the Russian armies was to succeed, Barclay's 1st Army was able to withdraw north-east on Drissa without being hard pressed. Bagration's 2nd Army was similarly allowed to pull back at its own pace, and this lack of enemy pressure led to great frustration in all ranks of the Russian army, all of whom were convinced that they could take on the invaders and thrash them.

The cause for the disappointingly slow progress of the invasion was the extremely hot weather and the light, sandy soil through which the thick columns had to march. The men trudged through a permanent, dense cloud of dust, slipping and sliding in the sand. Added to this was the scarcity of food, forage, and drinking water as the Russian rearguard carried off or destroyed all the supplies and spoiled all the wells with animal carcasses and other rubbish. The supply system, on which Napoleon had lavished so much care and attention, had also failed completely long before the Niemen crossing. It was a system based on huge, static magazines and vast, lumbering supply columns. The magazines had been filled with supplies gathered in from the surrounding countryside during the past months. Such vast demands on a poor and thinly populated area had used up every surplus, and the natives were now staring starvation in the face. These magazines, however, were for use only by the French regiments; all other national contingents had to fend for themselves; the French high command ordered them to requisition the food they needed from the already empty countryside. This Machiavellian policy had two totally predictable results: food could be obtained only by violence, and all the blame for such outrages could conveniently be laid at the door of the non-French regiments.

The Württemberg Cavalry General Wilhelm von Wöllwarth was caught up in this disaster and had to justify his contingent's actions in the following report to his monarch.

> On entry into Poland the magazines established there were closed to our cavalry; even in the remote staging posts no provision had been made for troops moving through. Also, our advancing army corps had already consumed most of the supplies that they had brought with them and to my cavalry division fell the unhappy lot of having to shift for themselves in a Poland already hostile to Germans.
>
> As is well known, the Polish peasants have little enough for themselves and that which they had they were forced to give to the French magazines long before our entry into their country. Here [in Pagosz] the French magazines in the area were closed to our troops. I sent Commissar Crais to the magazines many times which helped not a bit as he was told that these supplies were for the use of passing Guard and French troops only. Thus here also, supply on a self-help basis was necessary.
>
> On 30 May I received a personal order from the Duke of Elchingen [Marshal Ney] in Thorn: on command of the French Emperor I was to collect enough slaughter cattle for the whole Wirtemberg [sic] army corps for 20 days and to arrange this with the Polish government. This requisition had to be completed by 2 July i.e. within 48 hours. I sent Commissary Crais to visit the Prefects of the districts to liaise with them as to the manner and execution of the requisition. Crais could find no Prefects as they had all gone to attend a reception of the French Emperor who was to pass through the area on his way to Thorn this day. Prior to this, the Over Prefect had informed Commissar Crais that he was not in a position to assist with the supply of food for the men and would have to give his district over to the discretion of the troops. The regiments now despatched whole squadrons with their Regimental Quartermasters and the necessary requisition orders to collect the 800 oxen in 48 hours. Apart from this, the regiments were instructed by me to maintain the strictest discipline. The unpleasant circumstances of this enforced requisition of cattle gave rise to a great lament by all the nobility and peasants of the area. None of them

came to me, however; they all ran to the Polish General Krasinski . . . who advised them to wait just a couple of hours when the Emperor would arrive and he would present their complaints to him. In a few hours the Emperor came to Iznoraslau, two posts before Thorn, where all the noblemen who had had their cattle taken were presented by General Krasinski with the explanation that the Wirtembergers [sic] were robbing and plundering the area which was, in fact, nothing other than the execution of the order of the Emperor himself and Marshal Ney to collect 800 oxen within 48 hours, which certainly must have appeared as plundering if the co-operation of the civil authorities was withheld. Krasinski troubled himself to increase this impression to the Emperor. . . . During the Emperor's stay in Thorn, the requisition detachments of Lieutenant-Colonels Palm and Harditsch . . . arrived (in Thorn) with the necessary oxen to complete the requisition; they were no sooner sighted by the Guard than all the oxen and supplies which they collected were taken from them by force. . . . We reached the area of Insterburg on 15 June and found the whole countryside full of Davout's corps and the entire Imperial Guard. As the II Corps [Oudinot's] had previously marched through the area, it had been so plundered that the colonels had the most extreme difficulty in providing for their regiments on 16 June which was a rest day.

I sent Commissar Crais into Insterburg, where a great magazine had been established, to get at least bread for us, which we had not seen since the Vistula, but even this was denied to us. . . . No Wirtemberg [sic] soldiers went into Insterburg; no reports of excesses (by our troops) in the whole area came to me. . . Prinz Neufchatel [Alexander Berthier, Napoleon's Chief of Staff] was supposed to have exclaimed: '*que la cavallerie wirtembergoise avait portée le désastre dans Insterburg*'. That this was brought into the area before our arrival by French troops is the truth; but that the Wirtembergers [sic] brought disaster into this area is not true.

Königsberg, 10 August 1812
Wöllwarth, General-leutnant

This report vividly illustrates how more than half of the *Grande Armée* had been condemned by Napoleon to survive in Warsaw and eastern Prussia for weeks, only by resorting to the traditional French method of 'requisition', that is, plunder, looting, robbery, and violence. Their allies quickly imitated their French models as the basic need to survive concentrated their minds.

This incident has often been cited by francophile apologists for condemning the conduct of the many German contingents in Poland in 1812. Wöllwarth's report is never quoted; thus, the true state of affairs has remained concealed until now. What were the Germans to do, starve to death or carry out the requisitions as ordered by their French masters?

General Krasinski
The Polish general, Krasinski (here as General-Commandant of the Chevaux–Légèrs
Lanciers of the Imperial Guard), was involved in altercations with the Württemberg
contingent early in the campaign.
By kind permission of the Polish Institute, London

The men and – more importantly – the horses were already weak and
long undernourished; their corpses lined the 'roads' in increasing numbers
as did abandoned vehicles and exhausted stragglers. In the case of King
Jérôme's group, chasing the 2nd Army, there was the added delay caused
by the extra distance which they had to cover to reach their prey. The
forced marches, the heat, thirst, and weariness all took their toll and, at
the end of the day, as the regiments staggered into their bivouacs, some
companies counted less than half their strength. As one Westphalian
officer wrote in his diary: 'What shall we do if we catch up with the
enemy now?'

As already noted, Barclay's 1st Army was withdrawing, very unwill-
ingly, north-east on Drissa; at the same time, Bagration's 2nd Army was
pulling back east-south-east on Volkovysk, south of the Niemen, thus
aiding Napoleon by increasing the separation of the two Russian armies.
At about this time, General Count Lieven (Russian ambassador to Berlin)
arrived at Alexander's headquarters; he bore some advice from Scharnhorst including: '. . . Never make peace with the invaders . . . use Russia's
vast size to wear down Napoleon. . . . The first pistol shot must be fired
at Smolensk.'

Meanwhile, at Alexander's headquarters in Vidsy, von Phull and Clausewitz were called to an emergency meeting with Prince Volkonsky, General Arakcheev, Colonel Toll (soon to become Barclay de Tolly's Quartermaster-General or deputy chief of staff) and Captain Count Orlov. A report had been received that Napoleon had outflanked Barclay's left wing. Von Phull, the detested foreign architect of the mess in which the Russian armies now found themselves, was asked to provide a quick fix to restore the situation. Von Phull's excited response was to point the finger straight at Barclay: 'This is the result of Barclay's disobedience to my instructions!' (Von Phull had sent Clausewitz to Barclay on several occasions urging him to speed up his withdrawal on Drissa, but Barclay had refused to be panicked and, indeed, was spoiling for a fight, as were his officers and men). Volkonsky's response was: 'That may well be, but what should we do now?' To which von Phull retorted: 'As you did not follow my plan, I cannot now take over responsibility for the solution of this problem'.

There was a tense and mutually bitter silence, neither Volkonsky nor Arakcheev offering any constructive suggestions and obviously enjoying this chance to bait von Phull. No one present could think of a viable solution, so it was agreed to do nothing and to await further developments! Luckily for Russia (and for von Phull), the report turned out to be false, and Barclay's 1st Army reached the Drissa camp unmolested.

Alexander's headquarters entourage reached Drissa on 8 July and rode around the fortifications. One of the Tsar's ADCs, Colonel Michaud, was an ex-Sardinian engineer officer who took great delight in criticising many points in the design and layout. Many others in the staff agreed with Michaud, and Barclay also warned against fighting a battle at Drissa, urging the unification of the 1st and 2nd Armies before becoming heavily involved in any battle with Napoleon. At last, at this eleventh hour, sanity prevailed in the Russian high command. The Drissa plan was abandoned, orders were given for the earliest possible junction to be made between the two armies, and the Tsar, finally realising that he was ill-suited for the role of military supremo, confirmed Barclay de Tolly in command of the 1st and the 2nd Armies, and left to return to Moscow to organise the war effort of his empire.

The strained relationships in the Russian high command were not helped by Barclay's appointment to the post of commander of both armies as Bagration was, in fact, his senior, resented Barclay as a 'non-Russian', and was violently opposed to the policy of withdrawal without a fight. The historian, M. I. Bogdanovich, gives us telling glimpses of what was going on in the higher echelons of the Russian command structure at this time, with quotations from letters that passed between some of the top players:

From Bagration to Arakcheev:

It's not my fault; initially we stretched ourselves out like a piece of catgut until the enemy fell upon us. Without firing a shot we began to withdraw, I don't know why. In the army – as in all Russia – all think we have been betrayed. I cannot defend Russia alone. The 1st Army ought to advance to Vilnius at once; what do we fear? I am completely surrounded and cannot yet say where I will break out. I am not inactive but my state of health has changed and I have been feeling unwell for some days. I ask you as a friend – *advance!* Russians must not flee. We are starting worse than the Prussians. I will find a point where I can break through, even with loss. For you it is insulting. You have a fortified camp in your rear, there are no enemy forces on your flanks and only a weak corps to your front. You must attack. The queue of my army has been fighting hand-to-hand for a whole day now. . . I cannot fall back on Minsk and Vilieyka because of the forests, swamps, and bad roads. I have no peace. As God is my witness, I am glad to do anything, but one must act with certainty and according to circumstances. You have withdrawn and I have to fight my way out. If I am not strong enough to carry out this task, it is better to relieve me of this burden and give the command to another; why sacrifice the troops to no purpose and without satisfaction? I advise you, attack at once. Don't listen to anyone. The bullet is a cowardly poltroon, the bayonet is bold. That's how I think. The wisdom of Phull!

Lament for the Tsar and for Russia! Why let the enemy dictate to us when we can beat him? It is very easy to give the order to advance; make strong reconnaissances with the cavalry and attack with the whole army. That is honour and fame! Also, I assure you, do not stay in the armed camp. The enemy won't attack you but outflank you. Attack for God's sake! The troops are brave! Orders were given for us to fight but now we always run away. Here you have my openness and dedication to the Tsar and to my Fatherland. If you do not agree with me then let me go. I do not want to witness the destructive results. You can fall back 500 versts if our destruction threatens. Now excuse me! I have spoken to you as one Russian to another. If you don't share my opinion then forgive me!

Between us, I have been extremely insulted by the 'Minister' [Bagration always referred to Barclay in this derogatory fashion] but he has considered things and asked me in writing for forgiveness. I have forgiven him, too, and treated him as a senior and not a junior commander. I do this – and will continue to do it out of dedication to my monarch.

Prince Peter Bagration, on the march at Katan village, 7 August
Received by Arakcheev on 15 August

Another letter from Bagration to Arakcheev, written on 10 August:
. . . For heaven's sake, you may send me where you wish – even as a
regimental commander – to Moldavia or the Caucasus, but I cannot stay
here; the whole headquarters is so filled with Germans that it is impossible
for a Russian to survive. You may send me on leave if only for a month.
By God, I'm being driven mad by all this to-ing and fro-ing! The army
has scarcely 40,000 men but it is stretched out like a thread and drags itself
to flank and rear. You can split my army into two corps; give one to
Raevsky, the other to Gorchakov, but send me on leave! I thought I was
serving the Tsar and the Fatherland, but it seems that I'm serving Barclay.
I confess, I don't want to.

At last, on 1 August, the 1st and 2nd Russian Armies managed to effect
their junction at Smolensk. They were in good physical shape and it was
decided to stand and fight. They numbered 120,000 men. This was not
to be the great effort to stop the invasion once and for all, however;
Barclay knew that he was still seriously outnumbered by Napoleon even
though, by now, the central group of the *Grande Armée* had lost – or been
forced to detach – over one-third of its strength and, from the original
305,991 men who had crossed the Niemen, numbered only 180,000 men
in the actual battle. It was to be a firm delaying action, based on the old
city of Smolensk, to gain time for the Russian army's train to withdraw
in good order further to the east. In fact, only 45,000 of Napoleon's troops
(including all the Polish V Corps) came into action against 30,000
Russians; the losses were 10,000 and 6000 respectively.

A clear and bloody check had been administered to the invaders;
Russian spirits soared and all (except Barclay and his inner circle) now
expected there to be a violent and sustained counter-offensive. Barclay,
however, was holding true to his concept of 1807; he ordered a renewed
withdrawal. On 19 August, as the bewildered Russian army sought to
disengage itself from the enemy, Napoleon, well aware that time and
distance were working against him, made a desperate effort to catch
and destroy it in the Battle of Valutina Gora (Lubino). On this day,
35,000 men under Marshal Ney fought against General Tuchkov I's
rearguard of 25,000, and again the French received a bloody nose, losing
8800 casualties to the Russians' 6000. The crass mismanagement by
General Junot of his VIII (Westphalian) Corps contributed greatly to this
second defeat. Russian confidence rose even more. Imagine the
frustration felt throughout their ranks when Barclay ordered the
withdrawal to continue.

Caulaincourt, a usually reliable source on Napoleon, recorded that the
Emperor actually considered halting the campaign for 1812 at this point.
Watching the retreating Russian columns, Napoleon mused:

By abandoning Smolensk, which is one of their holy cities, the Russian generals are dishonouring their arms in the eyes of their own people. That will put me in a strong position. We will drive them back a little further for our own comfort. I will dig myself in. We will rest the troops and dominate the country from this pivotal position and we'll see how Alexander likes that. I shall turn my attention to the corps on the Dvina which are doing nothing [a reference to the II and VI Corps, facing off against Wittgenstein at Polotzk]; my army will be more formidable and my position more menacing to the Russians than if I had won two battles. I will establish my headquarters at Vitebsk. I will raise Poland in arms and later on I will choose, if necessary, between Moscow and St Petersburg.

Indeed, a strategic pause at this juncture would allow Napoleon's tired and much-diminished army to rest, refit, reorganise, and integrate the drafts of young, scarcely trained reinforcements that were trickling in from western Europe. The shockingly inadequate supply situation could also be addressed, though it must be said that, without active – and massive – Russian co-operation, there was not the slightest hope of supporting the *Grande Armée*; the vast majority were already doomed to die of starvation whatever Napoleon did; it was just a question of where their bones would lie. One thing was certain: on any further advance towards Moscow, the supply situation would only get worse; the Russian army would see to that.

It is also questionable just how many more battalions could be squeezed out of the Grand Duchy of Warsaw and the newly liberated Russian province of Lithuania. On 28 June, Napoleon had entered Vilnius (its capital) in triumph just after the Tsar's headquarters had evacuated it. The town was decorated with the badges of Poland and Lithuania (the white eagle and the mounted warrior) and, that evening, a delegation of the local nobility approached Napoleon to beg for the confederation of the two states, to which he was only too pleased to agree. On 1 July 1812, a solemn proclamation to this effect was read out in Vilnius cathedral, and on 3 July an imperial decree was published nominating a provisional government with Bignon as imperial commissar. One of the first acts of this new government was to order the raising of five infantry and four cavalry regiments which were integrated into the army of the Grand Duchy of Warsaw as the 18th–22nd Infantry and 17th–20th Lancer Regiments. Prince Ronauld Giedroyc was appointed Commander-in-Chief of this embryonic army, and one of Napoleon's aides, the Dutch General Hogendorp, was given the task of supervising the raising and organisation of the new troops. Fine words and titles, indeed, but the tiny state had absolutely no funds with which to realise the scheme, and its

economy was in ruins through the effects of the war so far. A large loan
had to be granted from the imperial treasury for the purpose but men,
weapons, and equipment were extremely hard to find, and many of the
new units were never brought up to full establishment. His failure to
galvanise the entire Lithuanian nation for his own purposes was a deep
disappointment to Napoleon. Only the upper aristocracy and the students
rallied to his colours; the mass of the populace remained passive. Another
anticlimax was how few Lithuanians in Russian and Austrian service left
their posts to return home and join these new regiments.

When Napoleon left Vilnius on the night of 16/17 July, Hogendorp
was appointed Governor-General of Lithuania. Shortly after this, a
deputation from the Polish parliament arrived at imperial headquarters to
ask Napoleon to declare that Poland had been reconstituted as a political
entity; this he refused to do because it might have precipitated a rupture
with Austria, and this created a profoundly bad impression among the
Poles.

Perhaps the factor which tipped the scales in Napoleon's mind in favour
of a continued advance on Moscow was the consideration that the
Russians would benefit much more from a halt in the campaign than his
own forces would. The Tsar would be able to mobilise the resources of
his vast realm: raise, arm, and equip considerable new forces with British
aid; create a virtual desert through which the invaders would have to
advance; build belts of obstacles that would be stoutly defended; draw in
the armies from Finland and Bulgaria; and harry the exposed flanks of
Napoleon's long lines of communication.

There was also the Emperor's 'Home Front' to be considered; he was
not without domestic political enemies and, with the cat away in
far-distant Russia for too long, the games of the mice might get
dangerously out of hand.

On 19 August, Bagration wrote to Arakcheev from Michaelovka, just
west of Dorogobusch:

> Your Minister might be good in the ministry but he's no good as a general!
> . . . I'm losing my mind with rage! . . . Organise the militia because the
> Minister is leading our guests right into the capital! . . . The army is very
> much against ADC Volzogen; they say that he is more for Napoleon than
> for us and he is advising the Minister! . . . It's not my fault that the Minister
> is indecisive, cowardly, stupid, slow to make decisions and has all the bad
> characteristics. The whole army insults him. Poor Pahlen [commander of
> the III Cavalry Corps] is dying of grief and all are being driven mad with
> rage and sorrow. We have never been so depressed as now . . . I would
> prefer to be a common soldier than a commanding general at this time,
> and that even under Barclay. I have written the whole truth.

Field Marshal Mikhail Illarionovich Kutuzov, Prince of Smolensk, early in 1813

Kutuzov's decorations included: The Order of St George (1st, 2nd, 3rd, and 4th Class); The Order of St Anne; The Order of Alexander Nevsky; The Order of St Vladimir (1st and 2nd Class); The Order of St John of Jerusalem; The Order of St Andrew; the Austrian Order of Maria Theresa; and the Prussian Orders of the Black Eagle and of the Red Eagle. He also wore a portrait of Tsar Alexander I in diamonds and carried a sword of honour with diamonds.

These letter extracts give us some idea of the divisions that were ripping apart the very fabric of the Russian high command at this strategically critical juncture; the atmosphere is one of near mutiny. That the Russian army could give such a good account of itself as it did at Smolensk, after weeks of demoralising withdrawals, abandoning their homeland to the ravages of the horde of the Antichrist (as Napoleon was held to be by most Russians), and with practically no faith in their commander, speaks volumes for the high quality of the army and all its members. It also demonstrates how ineffective Barclay was at communicating his strategic concept to his junior commanders and even to the Tsar because all of Bagration's letters to Alexander's close adviser had had their effect.

On 18 August, General-of-Infantry Prince Mikhail Larionovich Golenishchev Kutuzov was appointed supreme commander in Barclay's place. His task was to revitalise and reunite the army, restore morale, and to offer battle to the invaders as soon as possible. Kutuzov was sixty-seven years old, heavily overweight, physically and mentally ponderous, and blind in the right eye from a wound received in the wars with the Turks. He had served in the army for fifty-two years and had 'commanded' at the Austro-Russian defeat at Napoleon's hands at Austerlitz on 2 December 1805. 'Commanded' is probably not the correct formulation because Tsar Alexander was present in his headquarters prior to the battle, there had been considerable 'helpful' planning input from the Austrians, and it is likely that Kutuzov would have made a better show of things had he been left to his own devices. He took over command from Barclay de Tolly at Tsarevo on 29 August, and let it be known at once that the demoralising withdrawals would soon be ended. Barclay retained command of the 1st Army of the West.

This was just the tonic that the Russian army needed and had been longing for; Barclay had been unable (or had not bothered) to explain his strategy to his subordinates, and his actions – as we have seen – had been interpreted as near treachery. At last, a true *Russian* was in command! True, he had appointed Bennigsen to be his chief-of-staff, but Kutuzov would be giving the orders; Bennigsen merely ensuring that they were promptly and effectively carried out.

The new, aggressive policy could, of course, not be adopted overnight; a suitable defensive position had first to be found to tilt the playing field in favour of the Russians in the face of the enemy's numerical superiority. But there was the proviso that it had to be found somewhere between the armies' present location and Moscow; to abandon the capital without a fight would be totally unacceptable to the army and to the people.

Interestingly enough, the thought of abandoning his capital had already occurred to the Tsar, and he had decided to bite that bullet if needs be. It was still a closely kept secret; it would not do to spread panic and dismay among the city's populace, but this mood of cold logic, of determination not to bow to the invader even at the cost of giving up his capital city, proved to be one of the greatest surprises Napoleon ever had. 'A good general may be beaten, but he should never be surprised.' Napoleon's own words; and now Alexander, whom Napoleon was convinced was still the shallow, vacillating youth that he had beaten so easily at Austerlitz seven years ago, was to prove that, in the strategic sense, he had matured immensely. This development had been matched by an improvement in the Tsar's will-power which was shared by his court, the army, and the entire Russian people. This new combination was to prove to be exactly the right answer to Napoleon's invasion.

There are certain similarities between the strategic situation prior to the Battle of Austerlitz and to that just before Borodino. In both cases, Napoleon had brought his army to the end of an extremely long and fragile line of communication; in both cases, campaign attrition had greatly reduced the strength of his army; in both cases, the enemy's army was still largely intact; in both cases, Napoleon desperately needed to land his legendary knock-out blow so that he could end the campaign, dictate peace on his terms, and get back to Paris to concentrate on the management – and expansion – of his empire.

3

Selecting the Site of the Battle

THE ABSENCE OF strong strategic sites in European Russia has already been mentioned, as has the need for one to be found west of Moscow. This meant that one had to be found within the next 100 miles (160 km) as the Bavarian cavalry division of Major-General von Preysing-Moos (one of Napoleon's leading elements) had entered Vyazma on 29 August, and the proximity of the capital (and the mood of the Russian army) ruled out the luxury of toying with flanking positions even had they been available. After some consultation, the choice fell on an inconspicuous, gently rolling stretch of partially wooded, partially cultivated land south of the hamlet of Borodino. Of course, many other potential sites had also been investigated by Kutuzov's staff at the beginning of September, but all had been discarded as being too weak or too easily turned. Borodino was the best of a very poor selection.

Most modern maps of the field of Borodino are based on that drawn by the cartographers William Blackwood & Sons, and included in the atlas to Alison's *History of Europe*, published in London and Edinburgh in 1848, and this is a perfectly accurate and reliable representation of the natural and tactical features of the area in almost every respect. Where considered relevant, I have amended it slightly to comply with a map drawn up in 1814 by the Russian Lieutenant-General Baron Tolem; such amendments are mainly in the reduction of the extent of the villages (Blackwood makes Borodino look like a budding township whereas Tolem shows a more credible hamlet of very minor scope), and in the size and location of the 'Bagration *flèches*'. On this last topic, both sources show three earthworks; several eye-witness accounts of the struggles for the *flèches* speak of only two, others say three. When reconstructing the *flèches* late in the nineteenth century (they had been practically razed to the ground during the battle), the Russians built two-and-a-half works: two large, arrow-shaped *flèches* facing west, with a much smaller 'V' to the east, between them and facing south. According to some Russian military history experts, the truth as to how many were actually built and what shape and dimensions they had, will probably never be known.

The selected site straddled the old and the new roads from Smolensk to Moscow, and measured just over 4 miles (7 km) in length. To the

The reconstructed northernmost Bagration *flèche* from the west
The flat terrain in this area can clearly be seen. The monastery was not here in 1812.
The Semenovskaya Redoubt is to the left rear.
Author's collection

northern end it was protected by the River Moskva (the name by which
the French know this battle) which flows eastwards towards and through
Moscow. The northern sector of the front was covered by the Kolocha
stream, meandering its way, between sometimes steeply cut banks,
north-eastwards into the Moskva. Because of these steep banks, the
Kolocha is an obstacle to any attacker at this point. The new (northern)
Smolensk–Moscow road crosses the Kolocha by a bridge between the
hamlets of Gorki – in the east – and Borodino; the Kolocha runs eastwards
to the south of, and roughly parallel to, the new road for the next 3 miles
(5 km). It is here so small as to be wadable at most points and is without
any steep banks west of its confluence with its southern tributary, the
Semenovka. This last stream runs across most of the length of the Russian
front but is no obstacle, in most places, to the movement of infantry,
cavalry, or artillery.

North-east of the village of Gorki is a 'peninsula' of land bounded by
the Kolocha and Moskva rivers containing the forest of Maslova. Kutuzov
and his staff believed that the main enemy thrust would come straight
down the new highway, and they concentrated their main forces in this
northern – and naturally strongest – flank. A series of earthworks was built
along the eastern bank of the Kolocha and around the northern – and
even eastern – edges of Maslova wood. Kutuzov sited his command post

on a prominent knoll by the side of the road just west of Gorki village. This spot is marked with a monument today. The knoll affords clear views over the surrounding countryside to north and west but the view to the south-west extends only about 2 miles (3 km) to the gentle hill on which the famous Raevsky (or Grand) Redoubt was built. The open fields then stretch away further to the south to the woods along the old Smolensk–Moscow road and Utitsa village.

The Grand Redoubt was 2 miles (3 km) from Gorki but the southern half of the battlefield, where all the desperate fighting was to take place, was totally invisible to Kutuzov and his staff. The Grand Redoubt itself is variously described by different eye-witnesses; all agree, however, that it was open to the rear, and thus not really a redoubt at all. The modern reconstruction is merely a low, straight wall and this in no way helps to resolve the mystery. The site is marked with a tall, black column with a golden 'pineapple' and cross on top, and Bagration's tomb has been placed at its foot. Some eye-witnesses' reports of the terrible struggles in and around the redoubt during the battle raise an interesting puzzle. They speak of a deep, steep-sided escarpment close behind (that is, to the east of) the earthwork into which their horses almost fell and in which battalions of Russian infantry were concealed. Having visited the site repeatedly between 1992 and 1994, however, I can confirm that no such dramatic feature exists; the ground falls away gently into the shallow valley of the Goruzka brook, and then rises again to the ridge on which a large part of the Russian reserves spent much of that fateful day. Some eye-witnesses report that the rear of the redoubt was closed with palisades; others say that it was open. What seems certain is that no *gabions* or *fascines* were used in the construction of this or any other earthwork at Borodino. They were built from 4 to 5 September in a hurry by the Moscow militia who were short of tools, had no knowledge of how to make such things, and there was no time to instruct them. They consisted merely of a shallow ditch, about a metre (3 ft) deep, the spoil of which was then heaped up behind it to form a rampart which was pierced for cannon. The soil is light, the works were not faced with stone or any other material, and they crumbled quickly and easily under the intense and prolonged fire of Napoleon's massed field batteries, the ramparts falling into and filling up the ditches.

The approaches to the Grand Redoubt from the west and the south are flat, open, and almost level. The dramatic painting, by V. Verechagin, of French cuirassiers in a mighty ditch, lined with *gabions* and in a landscape bordering on the rugged Alpine in nature, alleges to portray the fall of this earthwork. The picture is good propaganda but far removed from reality.

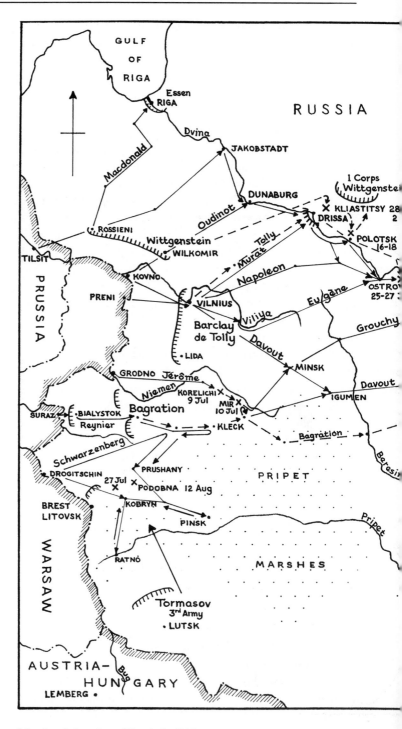

Napoleon's Invasion of Russia in 1812

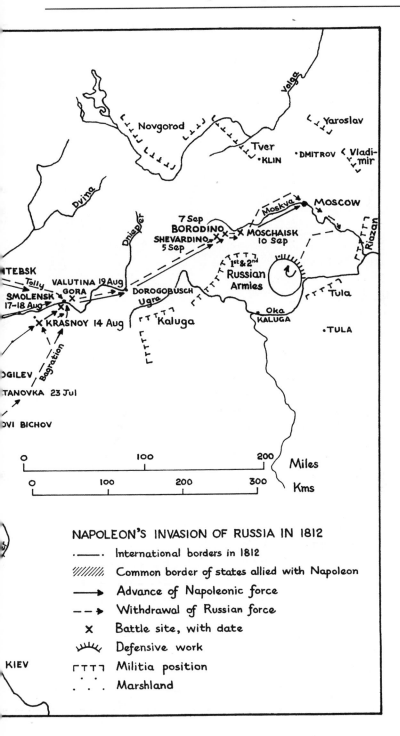

NAPOLEON'S INVASION OF RUSSIA IN 1812

.——. International borders in 1812

////// Common border of states allied with Napoleon

——► Advance of Napoleonic force

– –► Withdrawal of Russian force

✗ Battle site, with date

⊔⊔⊔ Defensive work

⌐TTꓶ Militia position

. . . . Marshland

Borodino church from the south
Time has passed Borodino by; it is still a tiny, insignificant little hamlet.
Author's collection

A little over a mile (1.8 km) south of the Grand Redoubt lies the site of the hamlet of Semenovskaya which was demolished by the Russians prior to the battle to provide materials to build an open-backed redoubt at the western end of the place. This work was sited on a slight prominence on the eastern bank of the Semenovka stream and looked into the rear of the Bagration *flèches* about 600 metres (660 yd) south-west of it. It was the site from which the famous panorama of the battle was painted by F. Rubo in 1912, and which may now be seen in the Rotunda in Moscow. The Grand Redoubt may be seen from this vantage point.

A red-brick monastery (The Saviour of Borodino) has been built in the middle of the Bagration *flèches* since the battle but the reconstructed earthworks can clearly be seen today. They are sited on a very gentle rise in the local terrain; they are (and were) completely open to their rear; the approaches from the west are flat, clear, and open. To the south, the woods – mixed silver birch and conifer, closely grown and in swampy ground – stretch away to Utitsa and the old Smolensk–Moscow road. To the east of the *flèches* the terrain was flat, open, and featureless.

It will be seen that the centre and the southern wing of the chosen Russian line were devoid of any significant natural obstacles except for the dense, swampy forest around Utitsa. Yet it was to be here that Napoleon's main attack was to strike home. The few simple earthworks which they threw up in great haste were far too weak to stop Napoleon's sledgehammer assaults, but the Russians exploited their defensive potential to the utmost, causing the attackers very heavy losses before being forced out of their ruins, or dying in them.

All the villages on the battlefield were tiny hamlets; just handfuls of primitive log cabins with some fenced-in gardens attached. Many were destroyed in the fighting; some were rebuilt. Others, like Aleksinki, vanished. The church in Borodino survived.

About 2.4 miles (4 km) west of the *flèches*, the Russians had built an isolated, very small redoubt on an insignificant hillock south-west of the hamlet of Shevardino. This work was out of range of the artillery in the main Russian position, and its exact purpose is unclear.

4

The Foreplay –
Shevardino, 5 September

THE ADVANCE TROOPS of the *Grande Armée* closed up to the western edge of the field of Borodino on the afternoon of 5 September: the main body on the new road; Poniatowski's V (Polish) Corps on the old road to the south. They soon detected the tiny, armed redoubt on the knoll between the villages of Doronino and Shevardino, and Napoleon ordered Davout's I Corps to attack it from the west and north and for Poniatowski to assault it from the south.

Defence of the work had been delegated to Neverovsky's 27th Infantry Division (of Bagration's 2nd Army) which had performed so well in its baptism of fire at Krasnoy on 14 August. The Russians had deployed the 5th Jaegers (of the 26th Division), 49th and 50th Jaegers in skirmishing order on the south bank of the Kolocha (here merely a rivulet) north of Fomkino and then south in the scrub along the eastern bank of the Doronino stream.

Flanking the redoubt itself were (to the north) two 6-pounder foot artillery batteries (twenty-four guns) south of Shevardino village, protected by two squadrons of the Akhtyrka Hussars. In, and behind, the redoubt were the Musketeer Regiments Vilensk, Simbirsk, Odessa, and Tarnopol. South of the earthwork were two more artillery batteries. Behind the infantry was Major-General Duka's 2nd Cuirassier Division (the Regiments Military Order, Glukhov, Little Russia, Novgorod and Ekaterinoslav). Further to the north, between Aleksinki and Shevardino, was a battery of artillery, and the Chernigov and Kharkov Dragoons of Major-General Count Siever's IV Cavalry Corps.

In the late afternoon, Compans's 5th Division moved off south from the new road, crossed the Kolocha, cleared the Jaegers out of Fomkino, and advanced in battalion columns to Doronino before turning east to assault the redoubt itself. At the same time, Morand's 1st Division and Friant's 2nd pushed south through Aleksinki, Friant attacking the Russian artillery and dragoons north of Shevardino, Morand heading through Shevardino itself. Behind the infantry was the cavalry of General Bruyère's 1st Light Cavalry Division of Nansouty's I Cavalry Corps. The rest of the I and II Cavalry Corps were following in support. All told, about 30,000 men of the *Grande Armée* took part in

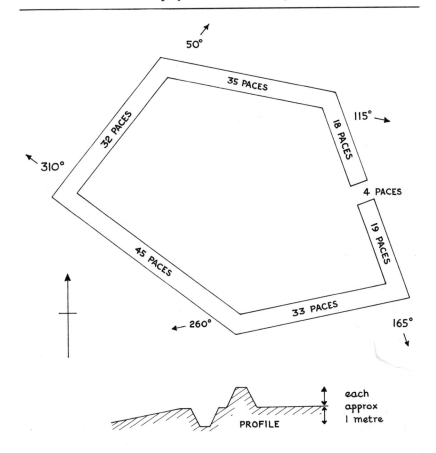

Shevardino Redoubt, 1993

this assault against initially 10,000 who were later reinforced up to 20,000.

Holzhausen, a German eye-witness, recorded 'It was wonderful to see the keenness of our soldiers. The beauty of the scene was enhanced by the magnificent sky and by the setting sun which was reflected from the muskets and sabres. . . . the troops marched on, proud to have been chosen to be the first to come to grips with the enemy.'

By this time, Poniatowski's Poles (fourteen companies of combined Voltigeurs) had reached Doronino and advanced towards the redoubt, pushing back the 5th Jaegers. A charge by the Kiev Dragoons under Colonel Emanuel restored the situation here, and, north of the work, the Akhtyrka Hussars caused the French infantry to fall back, at least temporarily.

Compans deployed his artillery twice during the advance: once on the high ground south of Fomkino, and then on a hillock only about 220 metres (240 yd) west of the redoubt itself. Initially the Russians held firm, a close-range fire fight developing between the 27th Division and the 25e and 111e *Ligne* to the north of the redoubt and the 57e and 61e who were to its south. For 45 bloody minutes the contest raged until Compans brought four guns up to within point-blank range and had them fire a salvo of canister into the crumbling redoubt. A charge by the 61e then secured the place which was found to contain only dead men.

Meanwhile, Friant's and Morand's divisions were forcing their way south on Shevardino village which was taken after a heavy fight. It was now 8 o'clock and the situation was beginning to look serious for the Russians but, at this point, Prince Karl von Mecklenburg's 2nd Grenadier Division (of Prince Gorchakov's II Corps), led by the fiery Bagration himself, came up behind the redoubt to stabilise the situation.

Now two columns of Polish infantry advanced against the left flank of the 2nd Grenadier Division; a timely counter-attack by Colonel Tollbusin and the Cuirassier Regiments Glukhov and Little Russia repulsed them smartly. The Cuirassiers careered on and took a battery of artillery at Doronino, cutting down most of the gun crews. Only three of the guns could be brought off. On the right wing the Kharkov and Chernigov Dragoons charged the 111e who rapidly formed square but too late to prevent the dragoons capturing two regimental guns. The dragoons swirled around the French square but without effect until the Spanish infantry regiment 'Joseph Napoleon' came up to drive them off.

As night fell the struggle continued, with the ruined redoubt changing hands several times; in the gloom, a battalion square of the 61e *Ligne* was broken and cut down by the Russian dragoons. By now, Poniatowski's Poles were pushing forwards along the old road against Major-General Karpov's Cossacks, and to the north strong French forces were advancing eastwards. The 'redoubt' had been completely destroyed, and an order arrived from Kutuzov instructing Bagration to break off the action and withdraw into the main position, which was successfully accomplished.

This pointless struggle for an insignificant and indefensible pimple of a hill had held up Napoleon for a few hours. It had demonstrated what tough opponents the Russians were and how bravely the French and their allies could die but, all in all, it was a waste, particularly when every man would be needed by both sides for the impending main battle. Barclay was disgusted with the affair as was Ermolov. Rumour had it – and there was a fair ring of truth to it – that Bennigsen had chosen to fortify and hold the site and would not allow the troops to abandon it without a fight so as not to lose face.

The day cost Napoleon about 4000 killed, wounded, and missing, and five guns. The Russian losses are less clear; Buturlin states: 'over 1000 men' which is surely too few; Thiers shows: '7–8000'; and Barclay de

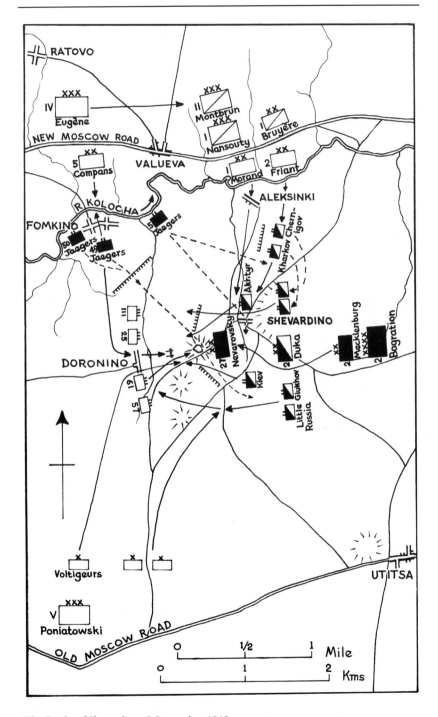

The Battle of Shevardino, 5 September 1812

Tolly gives: '6000 and three guns'. To Napoleon's astonishment, not one prisoner had been taken.

Considering the tiny size of the earthwork, the 'legendary reply of the colonel of the much-reduced 61e *Ligne* to Napoleon when asked by him on 6 September where his other battalion was ("Sire, it is in the redoubt")' must be taken with a pinch of salt.

5

The Calm before the Storm – 6 September

NAPOLEON SPENT MOST of this day in close and careful inspection of the Russian line, where much activity could be seen as they sought to strengthen their few earthworks in the little time still available to them. On two or three occasions, he advanced so close to the opposing positions that Jaegers took pot-shots at him. Napoleon was delighted to see that it appeared that his elusive prey intended to stand and fight at last. He recognised the natural strength of the northern flank of the Russian line: the close and difficult nature of the woods in the south and the invitingly easy, open approach directly through the centre, even allowing for the *flèches* there. If only the Russians would hold their positions for another twenty-four hours, Napoleon was convinced that he could destroy them; the battle he so badly needed was within his grasp.

Davout, too, had been examining the ground; he suggested to the Emperor that they should mount a strong outflanking sweep to the south with his own I and Poniatowski's V Corps (about 40,000 men), and drive the Russians north into the trap formed by the confluence of the Kolocha and the Moskva, while Napoleon's main body held them with a frontal assault. This plan was perfectly feasible and could well have succeeded but the Emperor rejected it on the grounds that it would divide his forces for too long in the face of the enemy. His refusal to countenance Davout's suggestion is surprising as such: an assault would have been quite characteristic of Napoleon in his earlier campaigns, such as Ulm.

It was the Emperor himself who had said in 1796 that he gave himself only about another six years as a fully effective commander. Perhaps his time in this role was now nearing its end but, as he was to prove in his dynamically brilliant, offensively defensive campaign in France in early 1814, he still had several top-quality shots in his locker two more years down the road.

It is most likely that his judgement at this point was affected by the cystitis from which he had been suffering for some time; or perhaps he was piqued that Davout had suggested a plan which was so good that it could – and should – have been his own? Relationships between the two were sometimes strained.

Napoleon's dispositions for the assault on the next morning were as follows. North of the new road were the IV Corps (mainly Italians), part of the I Corps, and Grouchy's III Cavalry Corps – about 40,000 men in all. Their task was to function as left-flank guard: to take Borodino and to assault the Grand Redoubt. South of the Kolocha, and extending down past the captured Shevardino redoubt, was the main body of the *Grande Armée*, Ney's III Corps, the rest of Davout's I Corps, Junot's VIII Corps, the I Cavalry Corps (Nansouty), II Cavalry Corps (Montbrun), IV Cavalry Corps (Latour-Maubourg), and, in reserve behind them, the legendary Imperial Guard and the Vistula Legion. This made a total of about 85,000 men. Further south, on the old road, was Poniatowski's V Corps whose task it would be to carry out a much-reduced version of Davout's outflanking right hook on the hamlet of Utitsa with a mere 10,000 men and fifty guns. In all, Napoleon concentrated some 133,000 men and 587 guns against the Russians this day: 90,000 infantry, 29,500 cavalry, and 16,000 artillery, engineers, and pontonniers – the remainder of his massive central army group that had crossed the Niemen.

The arm in much the worst shape now was the cavalry. According to Roth von Schreckenstein, the eighty-three French and allied cavalry regiments which fought at Borodino had crossed the Russian border with 47,460 horses and an average squadron strength of 140 mounts. On the day of the battle itself, they could muster only 29,425 horses; 18,045 had died of colic, starvation, exhaustion, misuse, or enemy action. Over a ten-week period, the average squadron strength had fallen to eighty-seven horses, and the quality and condition of these survivors were very poor.

The view from Shevardino Redoubt to the Bagration *flèches*
On the left is the monument to the *Grande Armée*. The monastery which can be seen is built in the middle of the supposed location of the Bagration *flèches* and was constructed in the mid-nineteenth century.
Author's collection

Prince Joseph Poniatowski
Generalissimo of the Polish Army 1807–13, commander of the V Corps in Russia,
Marshal of France in 1813, Poniatowski drowned in the River Elster while trying to
escape after the Battle of Leipzig, 19 October 1813.
By kind permission of the Polish Institute, London

This was particularly so in the forty-three French regiments, where good
horse husbandry was notoriously deficient. One eye-witness maintained
that he could detect a French cavalry column by the smell of the
suppurating saddle sores on the horses' backs, and Napoleon himself
admitted that 'the Frenchman is no horseman'. Of these forty-three
French cavalry regiments, only thirty-seven came into action this day as the
Imperial Guard was held in the rear, in reserve and out of range of the
Russian artillery. In comparison, forty-one allied cavalry regiments took
part in the battle; they were: seventeen Polish, six Bavarian, five
Westphalian, four Württemberg, four Italian, three Saxon, and two
Prussian.

Having completed his reconnaissance, Napoleon dictated his orders for
the assault on the Russian lines, which he planned to begin at 0600 hours
next morning. According to Tolstoy's *War and Peace*, (trs. Rosemary
Edmonds) Book III, Part 2, Chapter 27 these read:

> At daybreak the two new batteries established during the night on the
> plateau occupied by the Prince of Eckmühl will open fire on the two
> opposing batteries of the enemy [Bagration's *flèches*].
> At the same time the commander of the artillery of the 1st Corps,

General Pernetti, with thirty cannon of Compans's division and all the howitzers of Desaix's and Friant's division will move forward, open fire and shower shells on the enemy's battery, which will thus have in action against it:

24 guns of the artillery of the Guards
30 guns of Compans's division
8 guns of Friant's and Desaix's division
a total of 62 guns

The commander of the artillery of the 3rd Corps, General Fouché, will place the howitzers of the 3rd and 8th Corps, sixteen in all, on the flanks of the battery, that is to shell the entrenchment on the left, thus giving this battery an effective of some 40 pieces.

General Sorbier is to be in readiness to advance, at the first word of command, with all the howitzers of the Guards' artillery against one or other of the entrenchments.

During the cannonade, Prince Poniatowski is to advance through the wood on the village [Utitsa] and turn the enemy's position.

General Compans will move through the wood to seize the first fortification.

With the action fairly started on these lines subsequent commands will be issued in accordance with the enemy's movements.

The cannonade on the left flank will begin as soon as the guns of the right wing are heard. The sharpshooters of Morand's division and of the Viceroy's division will open a heavy fire the moment they see that the attack on the right wing has begun.

The viceroy will occupy the village [Borodino] and debouch by its three bridges [there was only one bridge], keeping on a level with Morand's and Gérard's divisions, which under his leadership will march on the redoubt [the Raevsky Redoubt] and come into line with the rest of the forces of the army.

All this must be done in good order (*le tout se fera avec ordre et méthode*), taking care to keep troops in reserve so far as possible

The imperial camp, near Mozhaisk,
6th September, 1812

From these, slightly obscure, instructions it seems clear that Napoleon had identified only two earthworks in the area of the Bagration *flèches*. Tolstoy is extremely harsh in his criticism of the Emperor's orders and reduces them to four orders, none of which could be, or was, carried out.

> . . . *first, that the batteries placed on the spot selected by Napoleon, with the guns of Pernetti and Fouché which were to come in line with them, in all 102 cannons, were to open fire and shell the Russian flèches and redoubts. This could not be*

done, since from the spots fixed on by Napoleon the projectiles did not carry to the Russian works; and those 102 guns shot into the air until the nearest commander, contrary to Napoleon's instructions, moved them forward.

The second instruction given was that *Poniatowski, advancing to the village through the wood, should turn the Russian left flank.* This could not be done, and was not done, because Poniatowski, advancing on the village through the wood, met Tuchkov there barring his way, and could not and did not turn the Russian position.

The third order was: *General Compans will move through the wood to seize the first fortification.* Compans's division did not seize the first fortification, but was driven back, for on emerging from the wood, it was obliged to re-form under a hail of Russian grapeshot, of which Napoleon knew nothing.

The fourth instruction was that *the Viceroy will occupy the village (Borodino) and debouch by its three bridges, keeping on a level with Morand's and Gérard's* divisions (for whose movements no directions are given), *which under his leadership will march on the redoubt and come into line with the rest of the forces.*

As far as one can make out – not so much from this unintelligible phraseology as from the Viceroy's attempts to execute the orders he received – it seemed he was to move through Borodino from the left to the redoubt, while the divisions of Morand and Gérard were to advance simultaneously from the front.

All this, like the other paragraphs of the disposition, was impossible to carry out. After getting through Borodino the Viceroy was driven back to the Kolocha and could advance no further; while the divisions of Morand and Gérard did not take the redoubt but were beaten off, and the redoubt was only taken at the end of the battle by the cavalry (a thing probably unforeseen and not heard of by Napoleon).

From these orders it might be supposed that Napoleon gave further instructions during the course of the battle. So not one of the orders in the disposition was, or could be, executed. But the disposition stated that *after the action has begun on these lines subsequent commands will be issued in accordance with the enemy's movements,* and therefore it might be inferred that Napoleon would take all the necessary measures during the progress of the engagement. But this was not, and could not be, the case because during the whole battle Napoleon was so far from the scene of the action . . .

While there is some substance in Tolstoy's criticisms of Napoleon's orders, in particular the wrongly sited artillery batteries opposite the Bagration *flèches* and the amazing lack of detail of the timings of the supposedly co-ordinated movements of the various corps, it is a well-known fact that 'no plan survives contact with the enemy'. Kutuzov's 'plan' could not be subject to the same criticism merely because it foresaw practically nothing except that the enemy would attack the Russian army in the positions it then occupied. It is of interest that both commanders stressed the need to create and maintain reserves.

Napoleon had also prepared a proclamation to be read to all the troops:

> Soldiers! Here is the battle you have so much desired. The victory now depends on you: we have need of it. Victory will give us abundant supplies, good winter quarters and a prompt return to our native lands. Fight as you did at Austerlitz, Friedland, Vitebsk, and Smolensk and posterity will remember with pride your conduct on this great day. May it be said of each one of us: 'He fought in that great battle under the walls of Moscow!'

It was one of those pugnacious, terse, but very effective addresses at which Napoleon, that ruthless and magnificent manipulator of men and nations, was so good. His army needed a boost in morale; they were not so stupid that the seriousness of their situation escaped their attention. Thousands of miles from home, in a very hostile environment, without even a ghost of a supply system, facing a determined and unbeaten enemy, they knew that the outcome of the coming battle was crucial to their survival.

It was not only the situation in Russia that was increasingly threatening to Napoleon's ambitions; he had recently (some sources say that it was actually on 6 September) received news of Marmont's defeat at Wellington's hands at Salamanca on 22 July, and this increased his need for some positive turn in events.

6

The Russian Dispositions

KUTUZOV DEPLOYED HIS troops along the selected line of defence as follows. In the north was Barclay de Tolly's 1st Army: Baggovut's II Corps (4th and 17th Divisions) with 10,300 men and twenty-four guns, was north of Maslova Forest; to his rear was Uvarov's I Cavalry Corps (2500 men and twelve guns), with Platov and 5500 Cossacks just to the east, south of the hamlet of Upenskaya. West of II Corps was Count Ostermann-Tolstoy's IV Corps (11th and 23rd Divisions; 9500 men, twenty-four guns) just north of Kutuzov's headquarters at Gorki. East of Gorki was Baron Korf's II Cavalry Corps (3500 men, twelve guns). This 'Right Wing' was commanded by General Miloradovich. The hamlet of Borodino was held by the Jaegers of the Imperial Guard; the bridge over the Kolocha just east of the place was prepared for demolition but left intact.

The Centre, commanded by General Dokhturov, consisted of his own VI Corps (7th and 24th Divisions; 9900 men, twenty-four guns) between

The monument at Gorki
Supposedly set up at the site of Kutuzov's headquarters on 7 September, the hillock commands quite a good view to the west and south. The mile post indicates that Smolensk is 275 versts [182 miles (293 km)] away.
Author's collection

the Stenze stream and the Grand Redoubt with Count Pahlen's III Cavalry Corps (3700 men, twelve guns) close behind it. Because Pahlen was sick this day, Baron Korf commanded this formation as well.

The common Reserve of the Right Wing and the Centre was located just east of the hamlet of Kniaskovo, and consisted of General Lavrov's V Corps (13,000 men of the Guard infantry and the combined grenadiers of the I and III Corps), General Borozdin II's 1st Cuirassier Division (2400 men) and a massive artillery reserve of 300 guns under General Kutaisov; 1 pionier and 2 pontonnier companies, a total of 8400 men. This artillery reserve represented 50 per cent of the total Russian guns present this day – a terrible weapon if correctly used. As we shall see, it was not.

The Left Wing (Prince Bagration's 2nd Army): Raevsky's VII Corps (12th and 26th Divisions; 10,800 men, twenty-four guns) was entrusted with the defence of the Grand Redoubt. To his south Borozdin I's VIII Corps occupied the Bagration *flèches* with 11,200 men and twenty-four guns. Just east of the VII Corps was Count Sievers I's IV Cavalry Corps with 3800 men and twelve guns.

The Reserve of the Left Wing, just south-east of the demolished village of Semenovskaya, consisted of Count Vorontsov's Combined Grenadier Division (2100 men), General Duka's 2nd Cuirassier Division (2300 men) and the artillery (eighty-four guns, one pionier, and one pontonnier company; 2400 men).

To the south, in the woods north of Utitsa was General Tuchkov's III Corps (1st Grenadier Division and 3rd Division; 8000 men and seventy-two guns). On the extreme southern flank, in the woods south-east of Utitsa, was General Karpov's detachment of 10,000 militia from Moscow and Smolensk, and 1500 Cossacks.

There is an anecdote surrounding Karpov's command and its actual location during the battle on 7 September which, if true, throws an interesting light on the state of communications within the Russian headquarters at even this late stage of the campaign. Kutuzov's original dispositions allowed the area between the Bagration *flèches* and Utitsa to be thinly held only by a screen of Jaegers (20th, 21st, 11th, and 41st Regiments); the old Smolensk road to be left 'open' with Tuchkov's corps in the woods south of the village and the road in an ambush position ready to hit the flank of any enemy force advancing eastwards along the road. Unfortunately, when Bennigsen visited the southern flank on the evening of 6 September, he heeded the concerns of the Jaegers about being left 'hanging in the air' and moved Tuchkov's command further north, astride the road. A young staff officer, Shcherbinin (who also knew the aim of the original disposition) was on site and witnessed the change but assumed that Bennigsen was acting on Kutuzov's behalf. The matter came to light, only by pure accident, months later in early 1813 when Shcherbinin asked Colonel von Toll (also on Kutuzov's staff at the battle) why Kutuzov had altered his original dispositions. 'It was not a question of His Highness changing his mind,' replied von Toll, 'there must have been some mistake in the way the orders were carried out.'

The question arises: did Bennigsen know of Kutuzov's plan? It is inconceivable that, as his Chief-of-Staff, he did not, yet he apparently changed this plan without even telling his commander or any other member of the staff. That there can have been such a lack of communication among the staff over so vital a matter, and that there was an apparent lack of written instructions, are unforgivable.

During the day, Kutuzov had the icon of the supposedly miraculous Black Virgin of Smolensk paraded through the ranks of the army to boost morale which, indeed, was high.

Kutuzov's orders for the coming battle are quite remarkable; we reproduce part of them here:

> Disposition for the 1st and 2nd Armies at Borodino, 24 August [the Russians used the Julian calendar which is twelve days behind the Gregorian calendar used in the west; it must have made Austro-Russian staff planning in 1805 an absolute nightmare!] Tatarinovo. In this order of battle I intend to draw the enemy forces to me and to act according to their movements. As I will not be able to be at all points during the combat, I place my trust in the acknowledged experience of the commanders and leave it up to them to act as best they see fit in the circumstances to achieve the destruction of the enemy. I place my hopes in the Almighty and in the bravery and cool-headedness of the Russian troops.
>
> I shall issue the necessary orders for the pursuit of the enemy and expect continual reports of the development of the combat in my command post behind the VI Corps. Husband your reserves; the general who has reserves is not beaten.

The astounding phrase here is: '. . . and to act according to their movements'; in other words, 'I make the enemy a present of the initiative in the coming battle'!

Kutuzov's advice to his subordinate commanders concerning the husbanding of their reserves was, of course, absolutely correct but the manner in which his army was deployed on the field made it a hollow joke. Unlike the Duke of Wellington, who made maximum use of every feature of his chosen battleground to mislead his enemy and to conceal his own forces from their view and fire, Kutuzov's dispositions placed almost his entire army 'in the front of the shop window'. They were drawn up in deep, closely packed formations in open ground so that Napoleon could see exactly where they were and how many (except in the woods on the south wing), and all Russian formations in the relatively undermanned and open centre section of the line (the unfortunate 2nd Army) suffered severely from French artillery fire from the early phase of the battle. His precious reserves were knocked to pieces for no good reason. No Russian commander at Borodino made any tactical use of the ground on which their regiments stood to reduce needless casualties.

Apparently the notorious Bennigsen had his finger in this pie, too. When the dispositions were being made, he recommended a dense formation as being necessary to prevent any attempt by Napoleon to burst through the Russian line.

If we compare the relative strengths along the battle line from north to south, on the morning of 7 September, the following picture emerges:

Grande Armée		Russians
on the new Smolensk road		
Eugène:		*Barclay de Tolly (Right Wing):*
IV Corps, Ist and 3rd Divisions of I Corps,		II and IV Corps,
III Cavalry Corps,		Platov's Cossacks
21st and 22nd (Bavarian) Light Cavalry		III Cavalry Corps
Brigades		The Reserve (V Corps, 1st
		Cuirassier Division and 300 guns)
		Bennigsen (the Centre):
		VI Corps
30,063	infantry	41,800
6,235	cavalry	12,100 (plus 5,500 Cossacks)
?	artillery	8,400
98	guns	396
in the Centre		
Napoleon:		*Bagration (Left Wing):*
Imperial Guard (part) I Corps (2nd, 4th & 5th		VII Corps, VIII Corps,
Divisions), III Corps, VIII Corps, I, II, and IV		IV Cavalry Corps, and a reserve
Cavalry Combined Corps		(Grenadier Division, 2nd
		Cuirassier Division, 84 guns)
55,757	infantry	24,100
19,300	cavalry	6,100
?	artillery	2,400
349	guns	144
on the old Smolensk road		
Poniatowski:		*Tuchkov I:*
V Corps		III Corps, Moscow and Smolensk
		Militia and Karpov II's Cossacks
8,430	infantry	8,000 (plus 10,000 militia)
1,638	cavalry	nil (plus 1,500 Cossacks)
?	artillery	48
50	guns	24

As can be seen, the great mass of the Russian army, condemned initially by Kutuzov's orders to a largely passive and reactive role in the strongest part of the line, was confronted by a smaller, holding force. On the southern wing, the opposing forces were roughly equal as the militia were armed only with pikes and axes and had no combat experience, and the Cossacks were useful only for scouting and raiding missions – they could not stand against line cavalry. In the centre, physically the weakest part of the line, Napoleon had massed his forces with a superiority of more than three to one against Bagration's hapless 2nd Army. One is tempted to ask whether Napoleon was handed a copy of the Russian dispositions before he deployed his army; he could scarcely have done a better job if that were, in fact, the case. It should also be noted that 15,000 of the Russian soldiers were new recruits, barely having completed their basic training.

7

The Battle of 7 September

NAPOLEON DID NOT rest well on the eve of the battle; very few of his army did. The vast majority had almost nothing to eat and only brackish water to drink. The tension of waiting for the dawn that would prove to be the last for so many of them kept all but the totally insensitive, the absolutely exhausted, the utterly fatalistic, and the few, fortunate drunks in nervous wakefulness. One eye-witness, von Linsingen, a captain in the Westphalian infantry, recorded:

> I was filled with the feeling that something powerful, destructive awaited us and this turned my thoughts towards my men. They lay on the cold, hard ground around me sleeping. I knew them all well; had so often received proof of their confidence, marks of their loyalty. How many of these brave fellows would not see tomorrow night? how many would be lying wounded and bleeding on the battlefield? I had the wish that the Russians would withdraw silently during the night without a fight – but the privations of the last few weeks had been too severe; better to end it all here; only the battle – a victory – would bring our salvation.

Captain Franz Morgenstern of the 2nd Westphalian Line Infantry Regiment recalled how, on the afternoon of 6 September, he had the opportunity to see Napoleon at close quarters for the first time.

> He was dressed in an open, light-grey overcoat, under this a green tunic on which a star was visible; white breeches, riding boots. On his head was his world-famous tricorn. He sat his grey Arab with the reins hanging over the neck and used both hands to hold his telescope with which he studied various points of the terrain in the direction of the Russian lines. . . . His peaceful, faintly yellow, marble countenance, the high, wide forehead – within which he was undoubtedly formulating tomorrow's battle plans – and the respectful silence of the high-ranking officers surrounding him (I recognized Berthier, Murat, Ney, and Junot) all made such a powerful impression on me that I could hear my heart pounding loudly. . . . Yes, truly, the close proximity of this extraordinary man wove a spell and made it clear to me how his French soldiers, bleeding to death on the battlefield, would summon their last strength to cry out a last *Vive l'Empereur!*

The Emperor did not sleep well that night, partly because of his illness. Very many others also had difficulty in getting to sleep, mainly because of the tension of the coming action. Morgenstern was a happy exception.

> Later that evening I met a Cuirassier who was looking for his brother in our regiment and learned from him that our 2nd Cuirassier Regiment was bivouacked nearby. I went over to their camp to visit Lieutenant-Colonel von Cramm, a boyhood friend with whom I had served in the army of Brunswick, We had not seen one another for years and our joy at meeting was great. With a bottle of wine and a hearty snack – the Cuirassiers were far better off than we poor devils – the time passed so quickly that it was late at night when we parted, each wishing the other the best for the bloody work of the morrow and that we might meet again, in good health, tomorrow evening.

Von Cramm survived Russia only to be killed at Quatre Bras in 1815. Morgenstern continues:

> My sergeant wakened me from a deep sleep before reveille; . . . it was 4 a.m.; a profound silence reigned. A signal gun was fired; all along the line, reveilles rang out to wake any still asleep. My company's roll-call revealed three officers, all the NCOs, eighty-one soldiers, and three drummers as being present. I had the corporals inspect the men's muskets and ammunition. Our regiment was already drawn up on parade when the order reached us to put on full dress as quickly as possible [this was often done for set-piece battles and usually involved putting on plumes, shako cords, epaulettes, and medals and decorations].
>
> Officers were allowed to remain in their blue, undress uniforms. After this had been done, the emperor's proclamation was read out before each battalion.
>
> This stirring address was greeted by the French regiments with the usual '*Vive l'Empereur!*'; the Württembergers responded with: '*Es lebe der Koenig!*' [Long live the King!] The emperor's words had touched the spot in all our hearts!

The French batteries opened up at 5 a.m. as planned. Their projectiles caused no damage initially to their chosen targets (the Bagration *flèches*) because the guns had been deployed out of range of the works. It was some time before this crass error was detected and corrected by moving them forward. It was not until about 6 a.m. that an effective bombardment commenced.

Morgenstern, with the Westphalians, commented on the early phase of the battle as follows.

The Shevardino Redoubt from the west
Left of the reconstructed, very small redoubt can be seen the top of the monument to the *Grande Armée*. The face of the earthwork which we are viewing is only 32 paces long. The main French assaults would have been from this direction.
Author's collection

> In closed columns, with bands playing and colours flying our corps marched forward into our appointed place in the line of battle. . . . We were in the second line behind the III Corps. Already, the first few hopping, rolling balls from a distant Russian 12-pounder battery reached us. This did not disturb the march of our well-drilled troops in the slightest, it was completed with the greatest precision as if on the parade ground.

In the III Corps was the 25th (Württemberg) Division. When it reached Gschatz on 1 September, it had already lost so many men (mainly to sickness and exhaustion) that its parade strength, with three brigades, was only 1456 men from colonel downwards. The decision was thus taken to re-organise it into three provisional battalions; each old brigade forming a battalion, each old battalion a company. To select the required officers, Lieutenant-General von Scheeler (the Württemberg divisional commander) lined them all up and strode along the front, picking out only the healthiest ones. All the others were grouped under command of Colonel Prince zu Hohenlohe-Kirchberg '*à la suite*' of the army; to follow behind at a distance to provide a pool of replacements for casualties.

The Emperor was up early; as the sun rose, he turned to the east. Never one to miss a dramatic opportunity, he gestured towards it: 'Behold, the sun of Austerlitz!' he declared to his entourage.

He had chosen to set up his headquarters just by the Shevardino redoubt, which was still littered with the corpses and other battle debris of the action of 5 September. At first, his view over the gently rolling, wooded landscape towards the initial target of his offensive, the Bagration *flèches*, was clear but the intervening 4000 metres (4400 yd) quickly vanished from his gaze behind thick clouds of smoke as soon as the artillery opened fire. For the rest of the day, observers at imperial headquarters had only momentary glimpses of the action, when the wind lifted the veil once or twice. According to most accounts, Napoleon, like Kutuzov in the opposing command post on the slight hill at Gorki, did not quit his position all day; both relied on incoming reports for their decision-making. As we shall see, it is possible that Napoleon actually did leave Shevardino even if only for a short time.

The Russians had deployed only about 300 guns along the front but these at once took up the challenge, pouring shot and shell into the enemy formations drawn up just east of Shevardino village. These were the 2nd, 4th, and 5th Divisions of Davout's I Corps who were to assault the *flèches* after they had been softened up by the preliminary artillery bombardment. As we have heard from Morgenstern, some Russian round shot fell as far to the west as the VIII Corps which was just south of Fomkino village. This would seem to imply that at least some Russian guns were initially deployed forward of the *flèches* because the maximum range of a 12-pounder gun in those days, to first strike on level ground, at 10 degrees elevation and with maximum charge, was about 3680 paces. A 6-pounder, under the same circumstances, would have its first strike at about 2680 paces. The range from the *flèches* to Fomkino is about 4300 metres (4700 yd). Even when a round shot was almost spent and rolling innocently along the ground, it could still inflict terrible wounds as many novices found out to their cost when they tried to stop them with their feet and were rewarded by having them ripped off.

Morgenstern's Westphalian corps was made up mainly of young conscripts (as were most other formations except, of course, for the Imperial Guard), and he related the following interesting phenomenon which took place as they stood for about an hour, inactive under the artillery fire:

> Already we had suffered casualties when my senior sergeant, who had seen much action in his past service in the armies of Hessen-Kassel, Prussia, and Austria, delighted me with his sense of humour when he came up to me and suggested that I order the three flankers next to me to stick out their tongues. This I did and was surprised to see that all their tongues were as white as their uniforms! I at once ordered others to do the same; theirs, too, were white. The sergeant assured me that this was the case with all men who were going into action for the first time. Of course, I had to put

this to the proof and demanded that he show me his tongue; he obliged immediately – it was lobster-red! 'And yours, captain?' he grinned. 'We'll just let that remain my secret,' I replied. The tongue test spread quickly to neighbouring companies and caused considerable hilarity as they were all white.

As we shall see, it was not only the Russians who incurred needless casualties by failing to take advantage of available cover from view and from enemy fire; some brigades of the allied cavalry were deployed in the open, along the Semenovka stream for hours before going into action; exposed to close-range artillery fire from the Raevsky battery [only about 700 metres (765 yd) away], they suffered heavy losses to absolutely no purpose.

The memorial on the Raevsky Battery, viewed from the existing bridge over the Kolocha
At the foot of this black and gold column is Bagration's grave. The picture shows how dominant the hill is for anyone in the corner of the Kolocha and Kamenka streams.
Author's collection

By wilfully ignoring the tactical opportunity to have their cavalry take cover, Napoleon and his intermediate commanders squandered much of what little remained of their cavalry assets. It would be fascinating to have been able to see what dispositions the Duke of Wellington would have made (for either side) for this unnecessarily wasteful battle. He was a past master at the tactical exploitation of terrain to minimise casualties and to mislead the enemy; he must have saved the lives and limbs of thousands of his men over the years.

8

Borodino Village – First Blood

TO THE NORTH of the Kolocha stream, Prince Eugène's command was advancing towards Borodino along the new Moscow road to deliver the first blow in the battle. It consisted of the IV (Italian) Corps, the 1st and 3rd Divisions of the I Corps, the III Cavalry Corps, and the 21st and 22nd (Bavarian) Light Cavalry Brigades.

Delzon's 13th Division (IV Corps) was in the front rank; the 106e *Ligne*, with four battalions, led the assault against the Life Guard Jaegers (two battalions) who were holding the place. The decision to hold Borodino, another (if slightly less exposed) advanced post, had been at the instigation of General Ermolov who convinced Kutuzov to place this regiment, almost unsupported, in advance of the main Russian line much to the disquiet of Barclay de Tolly. The Russians were apparently caught unawares by the French assault, and bundled out of the village and across the Kolocha with considerable loss in a smart fashion.

The Kolocha at this point is about 2 to 3 metres (6.5–10 ft) wide, 1 to 2 metres (3.3–6.5 ft) deep, and flows lazily along the bottom of a 'canyon' with walls (generally steep sided) up to 4 metres (13 ft) high. It appears that, in 1812, the bridge was some 50 to 60 metres (55–66 yd) downstream of the modern structure, at a site where the 'canyon' broadens out into a wide basin with low and gradually sloping sides where it would then have been easy to build a bridge with the limited materials and techniques available. A solitary *Verst*-post (mile/kilometre marker) stands today in the fields to the north of the existing bridge. On contemporary maps, the road is shown as having a distinct dog-leg at the old site, whereas the modern road runs straight from Gorki to Borodino, crossing the Kolocha at a point where the steep-sided banks are about 3 to 4 metres (10–13 ft) high.

The bridge had been prepared for demolition but the attack was so unexpected that there was no time to fire it. The victorious 106e rushed over the bridge, chasing the Russians up the slight hill towards two earthworks which were only a few hundred metres away from Kutuzov's command post. As the Life Guard Jaegers scrambled back across the Kolocha bridge, they formed an excellent target for the French who spread out along the banks of the stream and peppered their unhappy prey. Within about 15 minutes the Russians lost thirty officers and almost half their regiment. One of their officers, Löwenstern, reported that they were packed so closely together that every French bullet found a mark.

But now the 106e was to get a taste of its own medicine. Colonel Karpenko's 1st Jaegers (Bakhmetiev's 11th Division, Tolstoy's IV Corps) hit them in the flank as they were strung out in pursuit, and Colonel Vuich rallied the Life Guard Jaegers to take them in a frontal charge. The 106e fell back on to the 92e, who had also crossed the stream, and both regiments were hastened on their way by several discharges of canister from the Russian batteries in the earthworks. During the course of the action, General Plauzonne, the brigade commander, was killed; casualties in both regiments were heavy.

Barclay rightly forbade any attempt to retake Borodino; he had the bridge burned and withdrew the Jaegers into the main position. On the allied side, Eugène also decided that no further progress was feasible in this sector. He left Delzon's division to hold Borodino itself; pulled the rest of his IV Corps out of range of the Russian artillery at Gorki and in the Raevsky battery, and set up artillery batteries of his own to counteract them. It was just after 7.30 a.m.

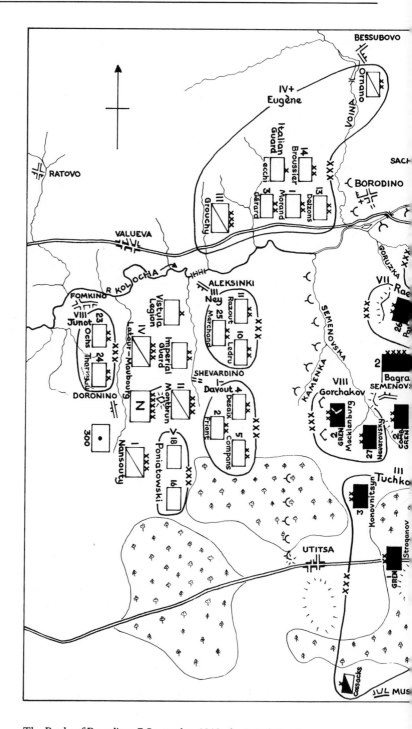

The Battle of Borodino, 7 September 1812: the Initial Positions

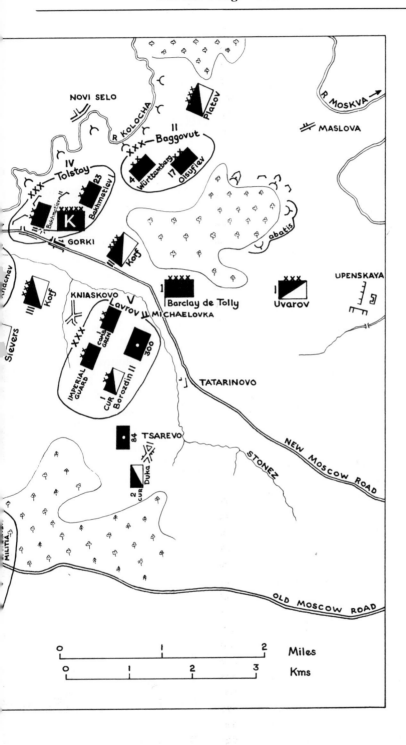

9

The Bagration *Flèches* –
Allied Accounts

AT ABOUT 6.30 a.m., Napoleon, hearing that the battle for Borodino village was in full swing and calculating that Poniatowski's V Corps must be making good progress through the woods on the southern flank towards Utitsa on the old Moscow road, ordered the first assault on the *flèches* to begin. Davout's I Corps was to lead the way with Compans's 5th Division aimed at the right-hand work. For this day's operations, the Emperor had arranged the command of the forces in the central sector so that Marshal Ney controlled all the infantry involved, and Murat, King of Naples, managed the cavalry. One effect of this arrangement was that Marshal Junot, commander of the VIII (Westphalian) Corps since the dismissal of King Jérôme, was left without a job. Junot's obstinate and erratic behaviour at the battles of Smolensk and Valutina Gora had deprived the Westphalians of any chance of earning Napoleon's praise on these days, and they had no regrets that he would not be with them today. Junot was, in fact, suffering from a mental illness; he died in 1813.

The garrison of the *flèches* was Neverovsky's 27th Division of Borozdin I's VIII Corps; in each work was a battery of twelve guns. General Prince Karl von Mecklenburg's 2nd Grenadier Division was in close support.

Compans had two objectives: the *flèche* itself and the woods directly to the south which were infested with the 49th and 50th Jaegers. In good order, Compans's regiments marched forwards into a storm of Russian artillery fire. It has been calculated that almost 300 guns of both armies exchanged fire in the intense struggle that took place in a sector of the field about 1.2 miles (2 km) square. The din was incessant, deafening; through it all the regimental drums beat the *pas de charge*, shells exploded, the wounded and dying screamed and groaned, officers and NCOs yelled commands, wounded horses thrashed about on the ground or careered riderless through the ranks.

Many eye-witnesses have recorded how limited their vision was at this point as the air filled with the smoke of discharging guns, exploding shells, and clouds of dust thrown up by the projectiles and by passing cavalry regiments. The chaos that reigned is difficult for anyone that has not experienced its like to comprehend; the shock to the nervous systems of those going into action for the first time was immense, numbing.

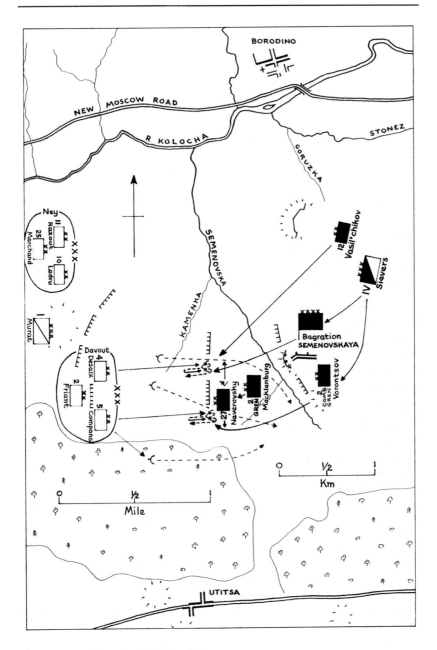

The First Assault on the Bagration *flèches*

At long range (up to 3200 paces) howitzer shells would start to land among the advancing troops. These were hollow iron spheres filled with an explosive charge and fitted with a primitive fuse designed to detonate the charge above or in the midst of the enemy troops. When the charge exploded, the iron casing would be split into fragments which would be hurled (according to the size of the charge) from 100 to 800 paces in all directions. In 1803 the British Colonel H. Shrapnel had much increased the destructive power of artillery shells by filling them with musket balls. Thus, instead of a bursting shell throwing off twenty to thirty pieces of its casing, the air in the vicinity of the explosion would be ripped apart by up to 100 deadly balls as well.

In the closely packed ranks of the men advancing against the *flèches*, the deadly mechanics of retaining the tactical cohesion of each company and battalion proceeded despite the random carnage. In such a situation, one round shot fired at close range (for example, a 12-pound ball at 800 paces) could cut down perhaps thirty-six men standing one behind the other. The golden rule was that such gaps in the frontage of a unit would be sealed again by having the survivors 'close on the centre' that is, each unit would concentrate from its wings towards its middle. By this method, the same density of men per unit length of frontage was maintained even if the overall length of the front was reduced. As is well known, the French favoured manoeuvring on the battlefield in column, as opposed to line, for as long as possible because such a formation was much easier to maintain in good order than the line, which was usually only three men deep. Wellington, in fact, reduced his battle lines to only two deep. This gave every man in the line the chance to use his musket effectively without endangering his fellows. In column, on the other hand, only a small percentage of the men present could use their weapons (the front two ranks and those along the sides of the column). Thus, column was the best and fastest way to move bodies of men around the battlefield as long as they were not under effective enemy fire but, once the column began to take losses, its commander should have given thought to deploying into line to minimise casualties. But even this decision was fraught with difficulties. The column (at least parts of it) had to halt, elements be turned to left and right, be marched to the flanks, turn to the front again, and advance into line with the foremost company. All this took time, had to be carried out at a deliberate pace in a controlled manner, and all this in the chaotic conditions described above. No mean feat for commanders or for men!

This time of transition was one of the most hazardous on the battlefield. The transitioning unit was extremely vulnerable to disruption throughout the manoeuvre; it was not organised to use its weapons, parts of it were marching in different directions, its members were concentrating on completing the formation change and not on the enemy, and all were caught in a stately ritual, a 'time warp' or mini-trance that paralysed their tactical readiness. The ever-present need to 'close on the centre' further complicated matters. If the enemy could take advantage of the opportunity to hit such a distracted unit with a cavalry charge, or with a determined assault with infantry in line, their chances of destroying it were extremely high. The history of the war in the Iberian Peninsula contains many examples of French columns being destroyed by British infantry in just these circumstances (Busaco, Barrosa, Albuera) and these were preceded by the British victory at Maida, in southern Italy in 1806.

Napoleon, of course, knew of the column's vulnerability on the battlefield, and sought to compensate for it in two ways: firstly, the enemy line would be softened up by a fierce artillery barrage; and secondly, the column would be preceded by a thick cloud of skirmishers whose task it was to fight down any enemy skirmishers, to further weaken the enemy line, and to prevent it interfering with column while it deployed. There seems to be ample evidence that many of the Emperor's junior commanders had not been made privy to this magic solution, or were incapable of applying it or unwilling to do so.

There were no such dramatic victories of line over column at Borodino; the Russian commanders lacked Wellington's advice, and where the French columns hit the Russian 2nd Army at the *flèches*, the superiority of their artillery and their greater numbers utterly overwhelmed the defenders of the works. The lightly built earthworks were literally blown apart by the convergent fire of the French batteries. The unfaced, unsecured ramparts crumbled and fell into the ditches, partially filling them. Casualties in the garrisons mounted dramatically as French shells burst among them. The Russians were mangled; their skirmishing line along the southern end of the Kamenka stream was forced back over the Semenovka (behind the *flèches*); their guns were dismounted, the limbers blown up, the teams and gun crews killed.

This is not to say that the assault was a cakewalk for the advancing troops. As they approached the works, they came within range of the artillery's then most effective close-range anti-personnel projectile – canister. Canister consisted of a cylindrical tin of the same diameter as the cannon's bore, containing lead or iron balls of various sizes, ranging from 1 ounce (28 g) to 7.5 ounces (212 g). At a range of 100 paces, tests – and battle experience – showed that, as a rule of thumb, half the balls thus fired would find a target if used against infantry. If used against cavalry, about three-quarters of the balls would 'find a billet'. At that range, the cloud of balls thus fired would spread out into a diameter of between about 4.5 and 7.3 metres (15–24 ft). The larger the balls, the smaller the spread. The horrific effects of such a weapon on troops in deep column formation may easily be imagined.

The Russian artillery officer, Löwenstern, witnessed it. 'The execution wrought by our batteries was frightful and the enemy columns faded away perceptibly despite the reinforcements which arrived continually. The more effort the enemy put into the assault, the more their casualties piled up.'

As the allied infantry advanced, so – battery by battery – did their artillery; continually reducing the range to their targets and increasing the destructive effects of their bombardment. Von Ditfurth tells us that thirty light French field pieces (3- and 6-pounders) were actually brought up to within canister range (about 500 paces) of the Russian *flèches*, an example of excellent co-operation between infantry and artillery in an assault. These 'light' guns were the regimental artillery pieces reintroduced into the French and allied armies following the capture of large stocks of cannon and howitzers from Austria in 1809. They had been in common use in all armies until about 1800, and were distributed among the infantry at a scale of two guns per battalion.

It was just before 7 a.m. when Compans's 5th Division approached the southernmost work. The artillery barrage had lasted about an hour. The French infantry threw the Russian Jaegers out of the wood and advanced at the *pas de charge*, storming over and around the ruined work and evicting the Russian garrison. A rapid and spirited counter-attack threw them out again. Not to be robbed of their prey, however, the French regrouped, assaulted again, and took the *flèche* for the second time. The fighting was fierce: the casualties mounted, particularly among the French commanders, who were often too close to the front line for their own good. Compans was wounded by a musket ball in the right shoulder (his twenty-second wound), probably from General Shakhovsk's Jaegers in the woods to the south. Then, in rapid succession, Generals Duplain, Rapp, and Desaix (commanding the 4th Division), who in turn took over from Compans, were wounded in their turn. Marshal Davout was also hit as the entire I Corps crashed against the two *flèches*.

The works had been built with no ditch or rampart on the eastern sides; any enemy forcing its way into the fortification would be fully exposed to fire from the Russians standing in reserve. It was not long before the French were thrown out again by the 2nd Grenadier Division of Major-General Prince Karl von Mecklenburg and the 12th Infantry Division of Major-General Vasil'chikov, this latter from VII Corps. General Ermolov attributed the fact that the Russians held on for so long in this sector against such crushing pressure to their superior use of the bayonet.

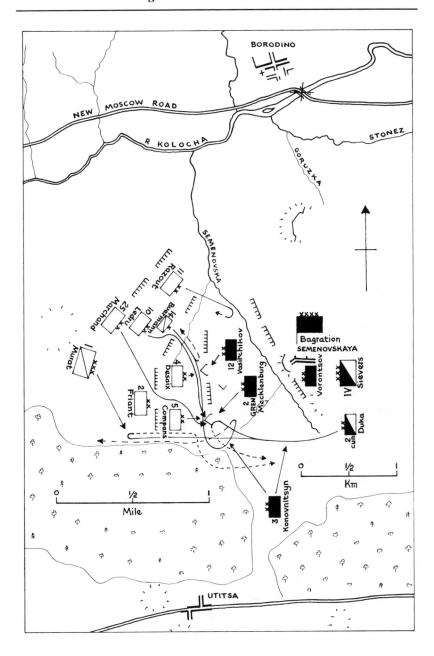

The Second Assault on the Bagration *flèches*

At last, some Russian reinforcements arrived on the scene from the north in the shape of General Sievers I's IV Cavalry Corps (Kiev and New Russia Dragoons, Akhtyrsk Hussars, and Lithuanian Lancers). With this 2000-strong force, Sievers temporarily broke the French grip on the *flèches* and drove Davout's I Corps back to the edge of the woods.

Ney now threw General Beurmann's 14th Light Cavalry Brigade into the fight to protect the southern flank of the III Corps as it advanced and deployed to aid Davout's men. Beurmann formed his brigade into three ranks; the *4e Chasseurs à Cheval* in front, followed by the two Württemberg regiments, the Leib Chevaux-légèrs and the Chevaux-légèrs Prinz Heinrich. He then trotted them forward abreast of the earthworks to charge. No sooner had this advance begun, however, than the Russian artillery poured a hail of shot and canister into the allied cavalry to such good effect that the 4e *Chasseurs* broke apart, turned on their heels, and fled to the rear through the Leib Chevaux-légèrs, taking this regiment with them.

Colonel von Falkenstein (commanding the Prinz Heinrich Chevaux-légèrs) quickly ordered his regiment to open up the inter-squadron gaps to allow the uncontrollable flood of fugitives to escape without taking his men with them. He then immediately charged the nearest Russian infantry mass.

While the 4e *Chasseurs* careered on to the rear, Major Count Bismark (commanding the Leib Chevaux-légèrs because the regimental com-mander, Colonel Count Normann, had been wounded and his second-in-command, Lieutenant-Colonel von Palm, had been killed) had the trumpeter sound the regimental rally, regathered his men, and joined the regiment Prinz Heinrich in a second charge. Fortune favoured the brave; with speed and boldness making up for their reduced numbers, these two weak regiments so imposed on the Russian infantry that their advance was held up for a time. Too weak to break any squares, and suffering continual losses from artillery and musketry, however, they soon had to pull back out of the firing line to seek cover in a depression south of the *flèches*. Their action had won time for Ledru's 10th Division (III Corps) to come up in support of I Corps at the hotly disputed earthworks.

The Russian infantry at once resumed their advance as soon as the Württemberg cavalry withdrew; Ney ordered a renewed cavalry charge to stop them, and a second struggle, more bloody than the first, ensued. Though both regiments combined now numbered little more than 200 riders, and despite the fact that their mounts were still half blown, they charged again, broke through the infantry, reached an artillery battery, and took two guns. At this point, however, they were hit in the right flank and rear by part of General Duka's 2nd Cuirassier Division, which had been called forward from its position just south of Tsarevo where it was part of the Reserve of the left wing. These five fresh regiments (the whole division was made up by the regiments Ekaterinoslav, Military Order, Glukhov, Little Russia, and Novgorod, and numbered just over 2000 men on fresh horses) charged straight at the tired Württembergers. Outnumbered and on exhausted, undernourished horses, the Germans stood no chance. Hotly pursued, they fled back past the south side of the *flèches* to reform out of harm's way.

Unfortunately, the 3rd Württemberg Horse Artillery Battery had just advanced into this area to support their cavalry comrades, and part of the victorious Russian cuirassiers flooded over them before they could unlimber their pieces or turn and flee. The Russians would probably have completely destroyed the Württembergers except for the simultaneous appearance from the west of Nansouty's I Cavalry Corps and the 25th Württemberg Infantry Division. Duka's regiments hesitated; their momentum was lost.

The other part of Duka's force had split off to the north, chasing a fraction of the Württemberg cavalry directly into the open throat of the southernmost *flèche*, held by the 57e *Ligne*. Mixed up with the few Germans, it was too easy for these heavy horsemen to break through the surprised infantry; with their heavy, straight-bladed swords they caused great execution among the Frenchmen, and soon the 57e began to crumble and to flee over the low remains of the shattered ramparts.

Luckily, at this moment, the three battalions of the 25th Division under Lieutenant-General von Scheeler reached the *flèche*. The 1st Battalion stormed into the work, taking many of the 57e back with them. The French officers quickly rallied the rest of the 57e and led them back to support the Germans. At the same time, the 72e *Ligne* of Ledru's 10th Division, III Corps, also reached the southern *flèche* so that the place was rapidly filled with allied infantry. The Russian cuirassiers were soon cleared out of the work.

During this dramatic struggle, the 2nd Württemberg Battalion had deployed into line south of the work and was pouring effective volleys into the mass of Russian cavalrymen swirling around in the throat of the *flèche*. It was at this point that the main body of Duka's Division, falling back in front of Nansouty's Corps, came up behind the 2nd Württembergers. It seemed that the German infantry was doomed to be cut down. The Russians were already in the act of charging into the unsuspecting rear rank when, in the nick of time, the Württembergers' commander, Colonel von Stockmayer, gave the unusual order for the third rank to turnabout. With admirable coolness and discipline the men obeyed. At the same time, the 3rd Württemberg Battalion (Colonel Pollnitz) and three other battalions of Ledru's 10th Division rapidly formed square west of the *flèche* (this was infantry's best defensive formation against cavalry attack). The Russians were now subject to a galling musketry from the front (3rd Württembergers' rear rank) and from their left flank (2nd Württembergers and Ledru's battalions). To add to the Russians' discomfort, the reformed Württemberg cavalry was now advancing into their rear.

King Joachim Murat, at the head of Nansouty's I Cavalry Corps, witnessed the conduct of the two Württemberg cavalry regiments; he was so impressed that he galloped over to them and enjoined them to charge under his command to try to retake their lost battery. They at once agreed and hurled themselves at the rear of the cuirassiers, joined in the charge by the mounted members of the battery itself. The Russians were thus assaulted from three sides at once and were forced to break off to the south, abandoning the guns. These were immediately taken over by their crews under Colonel von Brandt, redeployed, and brought into action again.

While this dramatic struggle was going on south of the *flèche*, Prince Karl von Mecklenburg's 2nd Russian Grenadier Division was advancing into the throat of the work intent on its final recapture by means of the bayonet, for long the favourite weapon of the Russian infantry. All their efforts were in vain against the determined resistance of the 1st Württemberg Battalion in the *flèche*, but the men of the 72e, who occupied the flanking ramparts [these have not been reconstructed] began to waver. Now the 2nd Württemberg Battalion, freed from the threat of the cuirassiers, climbed into the work to join their comrades. The fighting was fierce; General von Scheeler received a musket ball wound to the neck and was unhorsed. Though he lost consciousness for a time, he soon recovered and continued to lead his men on foot to such good effect that all Russian assaults were repulsed.

By contrast, the Württemberg cavalry, boldly chasing after the cuirassiers, became rapidly isolated and outnumbered when no support from Nansouty's cavalry appeared. They and the King of Naples were forced to flee for their lives back to the southernmost *flèche*. Here, Murat soon found himself in a critical situation, penned in by some cuirassiers against a part of the ramparts which was still intact and which his horse had no chance of climbing. He was saved by a troop of Württemberg infantry who, seeing his predicament, swarmed out over the ramparts, drove off the cuirassiers, and thus bought him time to dismount and climb into the redans, upon which they followed him. This event was immortalised by the Württemberg artist, Faber du Four, who was present at the battle.

The Württembergers and Murat in the southernmost Bagration *flèche*
This is the dramatic moment when the Württembergers of the 25th Division rescued
Murat from almost certain capture by Russian cuirassiers.
The engraving is by Faber du Four. Author's collection

The danger in this sector was not yet past, however. General
Konovnitsyn's 3rd Division of the Russian reserve of the left wing
(Musketeer Regiments Muromsk, Revel, Chernigov, and Kaporie, 20th
and 21st Jaegers) had been ordered up from their original position behind
the 1st Grenadier Division east of Utitsa village and, not only renewed
the assault on the *flèches*, but also threatened to break the communications
between Poniatowski's V Corps in the south and the main French body.

Part of St Germain's 1st Cuirassier Division of Nansouty's Corps now
arrived on the scene to aid the remnants of the Württemberg cavalry,
only to be smartly overthrown by Duka's victorious men who careered
on after them and captured two complete horse artillery batteries that
were following up behind the French cavalry. At this critical point, the
57e and 72e again began to waver; Murat, in the midst of the 1st and 2nd
Württemberg Battalions, his fantastically plumed hat firmly tucked under
his arm to conceal his identity from the enemy, raised the spirits of the
Germans (more than he knew) by encouraging them on with repeated
shouts in his broken German of: '*Ah, brav Jaeger, brav Jaeger! scheuss,
scheuss*'. Despite shaking with laughter [Murat's word '*scheuss*' or '*Schüß*'
meaning 'shoot' was pronounced like a rather more vulgar German
word!], the Württembergers preserved their marksmanship to such a
degree that all Russian assaults on the *flèches* were beaten off.

When one of Napoleon's adjutants appeared to find out how the battle for the earthworks was going, General Marchand, French commander, 25th Division, told him; 'Tell the emperor that the Württembergers have held a redoubt which was abandoned by two French regiments and have saved the King of Naples from being captured!'

It was not until about 11.30 that the struggle for the *flèches* was finally decided in favour of the allies. As the surviving Russians in this sector pulled slowly and sullenly back eastwards over the Semenovska stream, orders were given for the remnants of the captured works to be levelled. In view of the still-precarious tactical situation, the fatigue and scarcity of the survivors, and the complete lack of tools, it is most unlikely that anything was actually done.

At this critical moment, when the French right wing was in danger of being cut off, the VIII Westphalian Corps came up behind Nansouty's cavalry. Not knowing the status of the conflict in the confusion of noise, dust, and smoke, the Westphalians assumed that the body of cuirassiers bearing down on them was a Saxon regiment withdrawing to reform. The Saxon and the Russian cuirassiers wore very similar uniforms, with only minor differences, such as helmets, cockades, officers' sashes, and slightly different ciphers on the saddle furniture. It was only when the Westphalians saw how some fleeing French horse artillery men were cut down by the cuirassiers that the truth dawned.

The Westphalian Morgenstern's memoirs include the following comment on the event.

The thick clouds of smoke limited our vision so much that it was difficult to see the whole of our own brigade. . . . Then suddenly the din of battle ceased directly in front of us and a thousand voices roared out '*Vive l'Empereur!*' and we knew that our brave comrades had taken the redans. . . . A little to our left front a mass of black cavalry appeared out of the smoke and dust, bearing down on us with a thunderous noise. General Damas [Westphalian brigade commander] at once ordered the two regiments on the flank closest to the riders to form a six-rank-deep square by having their flanking half-platoons turn inwards. At once this was done and the riders were faced with a firm wall bristling with bayonets and ready to deliver a devastating volley. The cavalry, however, made no attempt to charge us but careered on at a fast pace towards a point somewhere behind us. At this point the general's voice rang out: '*Point de feu, ce sont des cuirassiers Saxons!*' [Do not fire, they are Saxon cuirassiers!] and no one fired. Moments later, we heard a loud argument going on among the senior officers in the middle of the square; some were saying that the brass 'A' on the black cuirasses stood for August King of Saxony, others thought it indicated Tsar Alexander of Russia and swore that they had heard Russian words of command. At this moment, these same cuirassiers came cantering

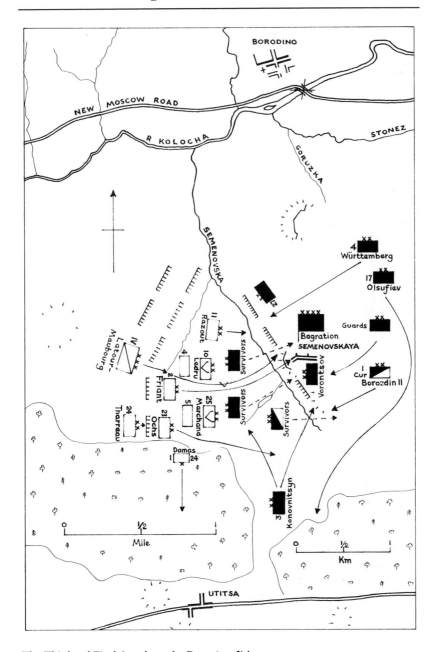

The Third and Final Assault on the Bagration *flèches*

back from where they had disappeared . . . still no one could bring themselves to give the order to fire on them as they completely ignored us again and rode past our square at a distance of about 15 to 20 paces. We would never have known the true identity of these riders had not one of them broken ranks (probably drunk) and fired his pistol or carbine into our square and then attacked two of our gunners who were outside of it. The volley that was then hurriedly ordered had little if any effect as the riders had disappeared again into the smoke.

A staff officer rode up to General Damas with an order for him to secure the communications between our centre and Poniatowski's V Corps, fighting in the woods to the south at Utitsa. We marched off as soon as the Russian cuirassiers had gone and our route led us past a scene of desperate struggle.

It was the moment when the reserves called up by the Russian high command arrived at the redans [*flèches*]. They were guards infantry and masses of heavy cavalry; their assault threatened to overwhelm the decimated and exhausted survivors of Davout's and Ney's corps. To counter this attack, Count Sorbier had brought forward a battery of eighty guns which wrought havoc in the ranks of the heroically advancing Russians. At the same time, Ney charged them with whatever cavalry he could scrape together to give the allied commanders time to reorganise their regiments.

All Westphalians (including our regimental artillery, which joined Sorbier's battery) took part in this struggle except our brigade which was marching off through the woods to aid the Poles.

Through the thick smoke to our left loomed two riders; one of them was our respected divisional commander, General Tharreau. He was supported by his adjutant and could stay in his saddle only with great difficulty; his sabre slipped from his hand. The adjutant called to me; I sprang to his side and he told me that the general's wound was fatal. He died later this same day.

10

The Bagration *Flèches* – a Russian Account

FROM LIEUTENANT-GENERAL Eugen, Prince of Württemberg (commander of the 4th Division) we have the following account of these dramatic events.

At approximately 3 o'clock on the morning of 7 September I returned to my bivouac on the extreme right wing from general headquarters. At 6 o'clock I was roused by a terrible cannonade from the left wing. The intensity of the fire indicated that Napoleon was bombarding the right centre in order to crush our forces before mounting an actual assault. But this was not quite true because his advancing forces suffered much more than ours did from the Russian batteries that lined the heights from Gorki to Semenovskaya almost without a gap.

A movement on the right, against our left wing near the Bagration *flèches*, where Prince Gorchakov II's newly formed corps stood (2nd Combined Grenadier Division of General Count Vorontsov and the 27th Division of General Neverovsky) opened the enemy infantry assault.

Compans's 5th French Division entered part of the fortifications but could not hold them. The struggle for these *flèches* went on from 6 o'clock until 10 o'clock. By this time, Gorchakov, Sievers, Neverovsky, Davout, Compans, Rapp (who had replaced Compans) and Desaix had been wounded and Reaumov had been killed. The bitterness of the fighting is witnessed by the fact that all the commanders on both sides had been hit.

Ney came up just after Davout with his III Corps (10th, 11th, and 25th Divisions) and their weight decided the contest for the three *flèches*. The allied troops then advanced against Semenovskaya but were vigorously opposed by Prince Karl von Mecklenburg's 2nd Grenadier Division and the 2nd Cuirassier Division. In this struggle Prince Karl and General Count St Priest were wounded, Grenadier Colonel Monakhtin, Prince Kantakusin and Count Buxthoefden [*sic*] were killed. Here the fortifications were stormed and Prince Bagration fatally wounded, but they were retaken by Konovnitsyn's newly arrived 3rd Division which had been sent up by Tuchkov I.

From 6 o'clock to 8.30 Miloradovich had been waiting for orders between Gorki and the Moskva River. At this point, Baggovut moved off with the four infantry regiments of the 17th Division towards Tuchkov I [i.e., to the south]; I followed him with the 4th Division and then came

Ostermann with the IV Corps (11th and 23rd Divisions). Four Jaeger regiments of the II Corps stayed behind Gorki to protect our right wing.

As Baggovut passed the rear of Baron Korf's II Cavalry Corps, he saw an old friend, Colonel Schubert (Korf's Quartermaster-General); Schubert wished Baggovut good luck. In response Baggovut grinned and began to sing: '*Marlborough s'en va t' en guerre . . .*'. Baggovut was killed by a cannonball wound in the lower abdomen at Tarutino later in the campaign. He was so fat that he could not see the wound.

Baggovut reached Tuchkov I at a very critical moment, just when Poniatowski and a Westphalian division were assaulting him. The 1st Grenadier Division (Stroganov) and the brigade of Count Ivelich, of the 17th Division, under Olsufiev managed to stabilise the situation and push the enemy back to Utitsa.

Another Westphalian column had advanced into the gap between Konovnitzyn and Tuchkov I; it was counter-attacked by Prince Galitsyn's 1st Cuirassier Division and Colonel Oreus's brigade and – according to Buturlin – thrown back with loss. Colonel Oreus was killed in this combat; Tuchkov I, Prince Galitsyn, and Count Ivelich were wounded. The struggle was vicious, both sides fought extremely well. As General Count Vorontsov wrote: '*Ma résistance ne pouvoit être longue, mais elle ne cessa qu' avec l'existance de ma division.*' [My resistance was not of long duration, but it ceased only with the existence of my division.]

Danilevsky's relation of the battle is very good:

Instead of cool decisions, the force of events dictated how we employed our troops.

Prince Eugen's account of the participation of his division in this epic battle continues:

General-Quartermaster Colonel Toll led me and my four line infantry regiments (still 3600 men strong) through the forest near Knjaeskowo [*sic*] to the centre where we were to plug part of the gap which had opened up in the Russian line. Some cannonballs reached us even as we were marching through the woods but when we emerged from their cover we found ourselves in the most dangerous of spots, right in the crossfire of the guns of the Viceroy and those at Semenovskaya. Shortly after this, General Barclay rode up with his entire staff to review the situation for himself. While he was speaking to me, Death reaped a rich harvest among his staff! Barclay, ever the epitome of icy cool-headedness and complete awareness, pointed to the Raevsky battery and ordered me to advance in that direction. The 2nd Brigade was in the first line, the 1st was in the second line. The first was formed into open battalion columns, the second *en masse*. We advanced to drumbeat. Suddenly, we noticed a great commotion in the battery, but before we reached it and could see what was going on, we were assaulted from all sides by cavalry. They were received with effective fire and, after making several ineffective charges, they fled.

Directly after this, Barclay rode up again, just as the enemy crater at Semenovskaya spewed fresh floods of lava at us. He told us that the battery had been retaken and, as a heavy mass of enemy infantry was advancing on the heights between the battery and Semenovskaya, he ordered me to attack this infantry and to push it back down into the valley behind it again.

I began to carry out Barclay's order to secure our left wing. It was like marching into hell. Before us was a mass of the enemy; the depth of their formation was unknown but their frontage alone was imposing enough. To their right-hand side was a battery of artillery so large that I could not count the guns in it, but the French reports say eighty, and everywhere there were masses of enemy cavalry waiting to cut off our retreat. To guard against this threat, behind the Infantry Regiment Volhynia (which was deployed in line) was – at each flank – one battalion of the Infantry Regiment Tobolsk in mass [like the French *ordre mixte*]. The second rank was formed by the 2nd Brigade at some distance, in columns.

We advanced towards the enemy through a hail of artillery fire. Generals Schroeder and Rossy were killed; hundreds of men in the Regiments Volhynia and Tobolsk were killed and wounded and within a very short time I had three horses shot from under me. As the last one fell, a battalion's adjutant who had just jumped from his horse to offer it to me, was also killed. The entire horrific, bloody scene was like a nightmare except for such events which convinced me that it was reality.

Despite huge losses, my division continued to advance; the enemy infantry fell back before us without a fight while our dragoons charged to take the enemy battery in flank. I now saw Barclay for the third time and must mention his utter resignation this day and the conduct of this most chivalrous of men who had been completely misjudged by Russian public opinion. He ordered me to halt and to deploy the 2nd Brigade more to the right-hand side where Miloradovich needed support. At this point, Miloradovich's adjutant, Bibikov, rode up and asked me to ride at once to his commander. I asked him which way; he raised an arm to point it out and a cannon ball ripped it off. He pointed again with his remaining arm and said: 'There! Hurry!' [Bibikov survived and later became the governor of a southern Russian province].

I handed over command of the 1st Brigade to Major Wolff (the only remaining unwounded field officer) and went to Miloradovich who was with my 2nd Brigade. He warned me that French cavalry was charging; Wolff's 1st Brigade had already formed a mass. Enemy cavalry also swarmed around Pyshnitskoi's brigade which had formed into battalion squares within which Barclay, Miloradovich, Raevsky and many others had taken refuge.

The enemy cavalry pulled back, their artillery opened up again and these regiments soon lost 300 men killed not to mention the wounded.

Apparently, the 4th Division (thanks to the independent action of Colonel Toll) was the only formation which, for some time, prevented the enemy from exploiting the dangerous gap in the centre of our line.

Buturlin, in his book, has me undertaking a much more aggressive offensive than I actually did. This illustrates his lack of knowledge of the exact details of events in two locations during the battle. Danilevsky fails to mention the 4th Division in the centre of the battlefield, which is odd considering their heavy losses. My belated report of the battle – and my absence from corps headquarters may have contributed to this as he worked from the official, submitted reports.

At about 6 o'clock M. Davout's assault on the Bagration *flèches* began. A lengthy cannonade by both sides preceded the actual combat for possession of the works. The decisive point for the allies was the advance of the III Corps under Ney and part of the cavalry under Murat. This part of the combat was in direct relationship with the movement on the extreme French right under Poniatowski against Tuchkov I. The combat took place firstly at Utitsa perhaps 30 minutes or an hour after the assault on the Bagration *flèches*. Poniatowski gradually won ground with the V Polish Corps and was supported by the VIII Westphalian Corps which was between the troops of Davout and Ney on the one side and those of Poniatowski on the other.

The combat at the *flèches* extended to the heights of Semenovskaya which were taken by the French after 10 o'clock or maybe later. On this section of terrain, within this time, the following French forces were engaged: first, Compans's 5th Division, Desaix's 4th, and the cavalry of the I, III, and VIII Corps and Nansouty's I Cavalry Corps. Then came the 10th Division (Ledru), 25th (Marchand), and 11th (Razout) of Ney's III Corps. Friant's 2nd Division and the IV Cavalry Corps were the last to join in the assaults on the Bagration and were active in deciding the outcome of the struggle for Semenovskaya.

Further to the right [south], against Tuchkov I the divisions of Krasinsky (16th), Kniaziewicz (18th) and the cavalry of the V Corps were initially engaged. Later the VIII Corps (Tharreau's 23rd and Ochs's 24 Divisions) joined the action here.

On the Russian side, the initial force in the Bagration *flèches* was Count Vorontsov's 2nd Combined Grenadier Division, the 27th Division (Neverovsky) and the IV Reserve Cavalry Corps of Count Sievers. Then here and at Semenovskaya, Duka's 2nd Cuirassier Division, Prince Karl von Mecklenburg's 2nd Grenadier Division and part of Vasil'chikov's 12th Division of Raevsky's VII Corps, of which four regiments were to the right of Semenovskaya and whose second line Prince Bagration drew closer to himself (to the left). From Tuchkov I's III Corps, the four line regiments of Konovnitsyn's 3rd Division were detached to the right (to Bagration) already at the start of the battle, reached Semenovskaya at a crucial point, restored the balance of the combat there but were then involved in the general retrogressive Russian movement which all troops here made between 10 and 12 o'clock when they withdrew about half a cannon shot behind their original positions. There they were taken up by the Izmail, Lithuanian, and Finland Guards Infantry Regiments.

11

The Raevsky Battery – the First Assaults

AFTER THE INITIAL action in and around Borodino, and the stabilisation of the situation along the Kolocha there, the Viceroy, Prince Eugène, redeployed his forces. In doing this, he was trying to execute his orders to take the Raevsky Battery. As the northern flank was too strong for him to break into, he withdrew part of his command to the west, crossed over the diminutive Kolocha approximately at the level of the village of Aleksinki (which has since vanished) and made a renewed advance to the east south of that stream. Some writers state that 'pontoon bridges' were used at Aleksinki; this is impossible and unnecessary. The stream here is so narrow that it can be jumped, and it flows through a very shallow, gently sloping valley. A pontoon [a square-ended boat about 6 metres (20 ft) long] would be much more of a hindrance than a help in such a situation. It does seem, however, that three or four small, conventional bridges were built to ease the passage of artillery vehicles.

The location of these bridges has also been the subject of some speculation. Some writers maintain that they were built just west of the point where the Semenovka stream runs into the Kolocha. Documentary evidence is very scarce on this topic but two facts speak against this as being the real site. First, the Kolocha here flows through a wide and deeply cut trench some metres deep; second, this site would have been only about 500 metres (550 yd) from the muzzles of the strong Russian batteries on the ridge in and around the Raevsky Battery. No commander in his right mind would have his troops build, or attempt to use, a bridge commanded by such effective enemy artillery fire. The site at Aleksinki is about 1000 metres (1100 yd) further away from these batteries and out of their direct view

Left on the north side of the Kolocha, to keep the Russian right wing in check, were the following formations: Delzon's 13th Division in and to the north of Borodino, and Ornano's light cavalry brigade as left-flank guard to the north at Bessubovo. The rest of Eugène's command (the Italian Guard, Morand's 1st, Gérard's 3rd and Broussier's 14th Divisions, and Grouchy's III Cavalry Corps) crossed over to the south side of the Kolocha and advanced to the Semenovka stream in preparation for the assault on the Raevsky Battery.

It was apparently about 9.30 before Eugène's artillery was redeployed and could open up a heavy bombardment on the battery to prepare the way for an infantry assault. The Russian forces defending this section of the front were Raevsky's VII Corps, whose frontage included the battery itself and stretched along the slight ridge to the south, to just north of the village of Semenovskaya. Because of the heavy fighting which had been going on in that southern sector since 6 o'clock, Kutuzov had already begun to detach forces from his right wing, and the VII Corps had sent two battalions down to aid Konovnitsyn's 3rd Division in Tuchkov I's III Corps in the woods opposing Poniatowski and the Westphalians. The Russian Jaegers were deployed in the woods and brush west of the Semenovka stream in skirmishing order, and the line regiments of the 12th and 26th Divisions were behind and to the south of the Battery in the valley of the Goruzka stream and on the plateau towards Semenovskaya. The 19th and 40th Jaegers had been sent from General Likhachev's 24th Division (Dokhturov's VI Corps) to reinforce Raevsky, and they were placed behind the Battery as was the 18th Jaegers of the 23rd Division, IV Corps. There was no infantry in the Battery itself as it was too small to hold them and they would have merely impeded the operation of the gunners. General Raevsky positioned himself inside the Battery as it gave him an excellent overview of the ground to his front, and he could be easily found by adjutants or messengers who might be looking for him. He gave orders that the guns were to be defended to the last, but seems to have sent the horse teams, and part of the ammunition train, to the rear to prevent congestion in the front line and to protect them from needless damage and casualties. There is also an account that he had sent the ammunition and teams to the rear so that, if the Battery were to be overrun by the enemy, they would be able to make only very limited use of the captured guns against the Russians. How he balanced this advantage against the danger that he might well run out of ammunition because of resupply difficulties (as seems, in fact, to have been the case) and thus be unable to stop an enemy assault, is not recorded.

Of Paskevich's 26th Division, the Regiments Nizhegorod and Orel were deployed to the right-hand side of the Battery, the Regiment Ladoga was on its left. Vasil'chikov's 12th Division was deployed in the second line. The 5th and 42nd Jaegers (26th Division) were in extended skirmishing order on the western side of the Semenovka stream, and had been squabbling with their French counterparts as soon as these had closed up to screen the advance of Eugène's troops.

Eugène's artillery bombardment was violent and effective, causing casualties, not only in the exposed infantry of the VII Corps, but also in

Pahlen's III Cavalry Corps which was standing about 600 metres (660 yd) further to the east on the plateau. The Russian artillery along the ridge replied, and the whole area was soon obscured by thick clouds of smoke that hid the advance of Broussier's 14th Division on the Battery which began at about 10 o'clock.

The advancing French pushed the Russian Jaegers back, over the Semenovka stream and up the gentle hill towards the Battery. As soon as the Jaegers had cleared the front of their own artillery positions, the Russian guns opened up with canister to terrible effect. This first assault failed in the face of the intense Russian artillery fire, and the survivors fell back to their start line.

Between 10 and 11 o'clock (eye-witness accounts vary) Morand's 1st Division mounted a second assault, supported this time by Montbrun's II Cavalry Corps to its southern side, and this time, aided perhaps by a slackening of the Russian canister through failure of their ammunition resupply system, they succeeded in taking the Battery, if only temporarily.

Just before this, Raevsky had received news from General Konovnitsyn that Bagration had been severely wounded and had been asked by him to go to Semenovskaya to take over command of the 2nd Army. This he refused to do because of the crisis that was building up in his own sector of the front. As he later wrote:

> This was a really decisive moment and I could not have abandoned my own position under any kind of pretext. My guns had opened fire as soon as the enemy infantry came within range, and the smoke hid the French so completely that we could see nothing of their formation or of their progress. One of my adjutants was standing a little to my left; after another salvo he suddenly cried out: 'Your excellency, save yourself!' I turned around to see French grenadiers pouring into the redoubt.

The charge had been made in the *ordre mixte*, and was led by the 30e *Ligne* with General Bonamy at its head, closely followed by the 13e *Légère*. The historian, M. I. Bogdanovich, has the 2nd Baden Infantry Regiment also taking part in this success but other accounts say they were attached to the Imperial Guard for the whole day, and no Baden account claims that they were at the Battery. A participant of the 30e in the charge described it thus:

> . . . we went forward at the *pas de charge*. A line of Russian troops, probably Jaegers, [according to Bernhadi they were the Infantry Regiment Poltava of Paskevich's 26th Division] tried to stop us but we delivered a regimental volley at 30 paces and passed over their wreckage. We then threw ourselves

on to the redoubt and climbed in by the embrasures. I myself entered an embrasure the moment after its cannon had fired. The Russian gunners tried to beat us back with traversing spikes and rammers; we found them to be truly formidable adversaries as we grappled with them in hand-to-hand combat. During this action many French soldiers fell into the wolf pits, landing on top of Russians who had previously fallen in. Once inside the redoubt I fought the Russians with my sword, cutting down more than one of them in the process.

Morand regrouped his division and prepared to exploit his success down into the valley behind the Battery.

Raevsky, who had injured his leg a few days earlier by impaling it on a bayonet sticking out of a cart, managed to hobble to safety out of the Battery and was forced to watch the struggle as an impotent spectator. So now, at only about 10.30 in the morning, the second major Russian bastion of the centre of their line (however inadequate a structure it may have been) had been taken by the enemy. Things looked very bleak for them, indeed.

Help was at hand, however. Just before the fall of the Battery, Prince Kudashev had ridden up to Kutuzov's headquarters at Gorki to inform him that Prince Bagration had been wounded and that the 2nd Army was in a critical situation. Kutuzov turned to General Ermolov, 'My dear fellow,' he said, 'see if something can be done to restore the troops' good spirits'. Ermolov galloped off to Colonel Nikitin, an artillery commander, and ordered him to come with him to the left wing, bringing three (Nikitin says two) horse artillery batteries. They then met Major-General Count Kutaisov, commander of the 300-gun Artillery Reserve of the 1st Army, who at once joined their party. As they rode south through the valley behind the Battery, they saw the bitter fighting going on there. Ermolov ordered the batteries with them to unlimber and fire into the French troops on the ridge; he then took command of Major Demidov's 3rd Battalion, Infantry Regiment Ufa and the 18th Jaegers, and led an immediate counter-attack. The 19th and 40th Jaegers supported him to his left-hand side. After a desperate, 15-minute struggle, the Battery was once more in Russian hands.

Ermolov's report to Barclay on this dramatic event (quoted in Bogdanovich) is of interest:

On 26 August [the Russian date] I was in process of carrying out Your Excellency's orders to go to the left wing to reinforce the artillery there. As I passed our centre, on which an eighteen-gun redoubt had been built on a hill, and the right wing of the 2nd Army of The West, it was already in enemy hands and they had put a strong garrison into it. Enemy artillery dominated the area around the hill and their columns were hurrying forward to exploit their success.

Our men were not only falling back in disorder in groups, they were fleeing with no thought of defence and brought the 18th, 19th, and 40th Jaegers – who were withdrawing in the best form – into disorder so that the enemy could consolidate his gains.

This height dominated the positions of both our armies; the eighteen lost guns were so vital that there was no doubt – the battery had to be retaken.

I decided to do it; desperation and luck were needed – it worked!

I took only the 3rd Battalion, Infantry Regiment Ufa, stopped the fugitives, and, with the men, clumped into a sort of column, I led a bayonet charge.

The enemy defended himself furiously; his artillery caused us terrible loss but it didn't help him. The 3rd Ufa and the 18th Jaegers charged straight into the battery; the 19th and 40th Jaegers went around the left-hand side and, within a quarter-of-an-hour the enemy had been punished for his temerity.

The battery was ours again and the hill was covered with corpses. General Bonami [sic] was captured. The confusion among our troops did not permit a pursuit. We held on to the battery until Your Excellency sent up the VI Corps.

In the battery I found eighteen guns and only one round of canister.

Gradually, all the gun crews were killed or wounded; I used the men of the Regiment Ufa to replace them and repelled all assaults for one-and-a-half hours. I then handed over the battery to the general officer commanding the 24th Division, Major-General Likhachev.

Just as I was setting off for the left wing, I was wounded in the neck.

Those who distinguished themselves were the commanding officer of the 3rd Battalion, Infantry Regiment Ufa, Major Demidov, the commander of the 18th Jaegers, Lieutenant-Colonel Chichakov, and Major-General Count Kutaisov's Adjutant, Lieutenant Posdiev.

Signed Ermolov, Major-General
20 September [old style]

The 12th and 26th Divisions had begun to pursue the enemy but Ermolov called them back as the French had now reformed and were too strong.

Perhaps the fact that Ermolov could find only one round of canister ammunition left in the recaptured Battery is why the second French assault had succeeded. As Count Kutaisov had been killed in the fight to recover the Battery, it is also likely that the failure of the Russians to make use of his 300-gun artillery reserve, and a continued lack of the appropriate ammunition in the Battery, were key factors in its eventual capture later in the day.

The fighting had been intense in and around the Battery and losses were high on both sides. Danilevsky, in his account of the battle, relates the following event:

> During the Russian counter-attack, General Bonamy was wounded several times by bayonets. To save his life, he shouted out that he was the King of Naples and this was believed at first. An adjutant at once rushed with this news to Kutuzov's headquarters. On hearing this, the Prince's entire entourage broke out in cheers; he, however, said: 'We will await confirmation'. The prisoner was eventually produced and the truth came out. Meanwhile, news of 'Murat's capture' spread through the Russian army like wildfire. Major von Heideggen of the 4th Jaegers heard it from a Cossack and Major von Wolff, of the Duke of Württemberg's staff heard it, too. Wolff told the Duke with the addition of: 'It will all be over before they call us up!'. How wrong he was to be!

12

Semenovskaya – Last Bastion of the Russian Centre

IT WAS NOW about 10.30. The battered survivors of the Russian left wing had at last given up the struggle to hold the *flèches* and had pulled back eastwards about 300 paces across the Semenovka stream and behind the burning ruins of what had once been the hamlet of Semenovskaya. At the western end of the place a redoubt had been built which was slightly higher than the *flèches* and overlooked them. [On a clear day it would be possible to see Semenovskaya from the Raevsky Battery.]

Meerheim, a Saxon cavalry officer, described the scene as Lorge's 7th Heavy Cavalry Division of Latour-Maubourg's IV Cavalry Corps advanced to the attack:

> It must now have been about 7 o'clock when it came to be our turn to prove ourselves in this great battle. In the same order as hitherto we moved down the slope and trotted towards the next one. The first artillery shot landed in our ranks but, as we crested the slight ridge, we saw the entire battle for the centre laid out before our eyes. All was hidden in thick clouds of smoke; a dense mass of men and horses could be seen, rolling backwards and forwards on the enemy's ridge; the air was filled with the roar of hundreds of cannon and the rattle of musketry.
>
> We kept our direction on the burning village [Semenovskaya] unchanged and were fairly close to its batteries. Before us was the mass of the infantry of Marshal Ney's (III) Corps who seemed to be in the act of storming the enemy-held heights. We followed slowly, halting now and then, but as the enemy gunfire began to become more effective – not only from the battery to our front but also from other batteries to the sides – we were caught in a cross-fire. We thus made some movements to the side, without losing sight of the burning village which was our original target, in the apparent hope of finding some dead ground in which to shelter from the enemy artillery fire, but we could find none as all the heights ahead of us were lined with Russian guns. Our losses mounted as we approached the enemy line.
>
> As we came into the effective range of their canister, we saw that the throng of the French infantry in front of us was suddenly thrown into high activity and although much was still clouded in smoke, the wild shouts of the combatants told us that they were at each other's throats. Shortly after

this, Ney's men fell back to either side of our column without being followed by the Russians, who remained in position on the ridge. A hail of all sorts of artillery projectiles soon made us aware that we were now the only worthwhile target in range of the Russian guns. We would rather have attacked at once than endure this torture passively.

At this point we were a few hundred paces from the foot of the steep slope which led up to the burning village of Semenovskaya with its batteries, redoubts, and masses of infantry. In front of us the ground fell away down a gentle slope into a shallow, flat-bottomed valley, which ran parallel to our front and was filled with bushes to our right, in the direction of the site of the nearby battleground on which Davout and Poniatowski were fighting, as the billowing smoke and the wild cries from this direction told us.

To our left, this valley led to where the King of Naples was assaulting the enemy centre; from the noise which we could hear, the fighting was just as bitter there as in the south.

Now, just when the artillery fire was becoming unbearable, *Sousleutnant* Baron von Biedermann (ADC to Latour-Maubourg) opened the list of officers of the brigade killed in action when a canister ball smashed into his chest. Shortly after this, Colonel von Truetzschler and *Sousleutnant* von Hagen dropped from their horses badly wounded, and General Maubourg's horse was killed under him. Death reaped a rich harvest in the lines behind us as well. Major-General von Lepel (commander of the Westphalian Heavy Cavalry Brigade) sank to the ground fatally wounded. He died with the name of the Queen of Westphalia – whom he adored – on his lips. [This eye-witness account of Lepel's death refutes the other report that he was wounded much later during the fighting in Semenovskaya itself.]

The commander of the 1st Westphalian Cuirassier Regiment, Colonel von Gilsa, was killed shortly afterwards.

As we still failed to grasp the nettle and charge the enemy, we suffered accordingly without being able to avenge ourselves. The cause of our delay was the extreme difficulty of getting at them, as the slope up which we would have to charge seemed to be too steep to scale. The slope was steep but cut through in many places with narrow, deeply worn paths leading upwards at angles, but there seemed to be none in the section before us, in front of the village. The only thing to do was to try to ride up the slope diagonally. We thus advanced across the valley floor at an angle, but when we arrived at the foot of the slope, it was unclimbable. The situation left us no time to ponder the problem, we just charged at it at a gallop, our reins over the horses' necks and our spurs in their flanks. The vertical height we had to scale was about 20 *elles* [1 Saxon *elle* = 56 centimetres (22 in)] but the gradient was so steep that those who failed to tackle it diagonally frequently fell over backwards and were trampled by those coming behind.

Once at the top, we saw before us the burnt-out village of

Semenovskaya, about 60 paces away and marked now only by some remaining glowing beams. Directly in front of the village, covering the point at which we had scaled the slope, was a strong square made up of several infantry battalions and a strong battery. To our left, covering the right flank of the village, and beyond it, were several more such squares set up in a chessboard formation. One of these, the one furthest to the rear, was of great size.

The Gardes du Corps at once charged the nearest enemy square; the Zastrow Cuirassiers followed as fast as they could. The first square was cut down and the battery next to the redoubt taken despite furious Russian resistance. Without reforming, the wild chase went on towards the other infantry squares to the left and rear who thought they were covered by the burning ruins of Semenovskaya and who directed a violent hail of musketry against us. But nothing could stop us, so mad were we; we charged straight on through the burning ruins towards the Russians who awaited us with levelled bayonets. It was here that our losses mounted as several riders and their horses crashed through the charred floor timbers and into the many storage cellars below. Scarcely through this peril, we found ourselves in the midst of the enemy infantry and at once began a bloody butchery, fought by both sides with bitter fury. The bayonets emptied several of our saddles but we exacted a threefold revenge with our swords. Scarcely was one square cut down than we came upon the next and so the murderous work went on.

This vivid portrayal of the desperate noise and confusion of close combat would not have been popular with the Duke of Wellington. He was a very cool and controlled character, who was frequently quoted as being very critical of his British cavalry regiments in the Peninsular War, where he condemned them on one occasion as being 'good for nothing but galloping'.

Another witness to such a cavalry combat (later this day) was Colonel Schubert, Quartermaster-General of the II Russian Cavalry Corps:

It is impossible to imagine the chaos and confusion unless you have seen it yourself. Of command and control there was no trace. Each regiment gathered itself in recall and charged the enemy again at once. All the regiments were mixed up together, slashing and cutting at the foe in the midst of the ruins of our infantry which was trying to reorganise itself as quickly as possible.

Paskevich was cursing and tearing out his hair. Barclay de Tolly's horse had been killed and he was calmly trying to restore order on foot.

Suddenly, up charged a Saxon Cuirassier regiment which had broken through our left wing, assaulted our guards infantry squares, been repulsed, and was now trying to escape through our second and third lines.

There was thick dust everywhere, no one could see more than 10 feet [3 m].

The opposing artillery batteries both fired into this confused mass, regardless of whether they hit friend or foe.

Roth von Schreckenstein reinforces the case that once cavalry has been committed to combat, any hope of managing it is gone:

> The chances of controlling or stopping a cavalry regiment in such circumstances belong in the realms of pious hopes. Men with courage (the real cavalry spirit) will pursue and attack the enemy for as long as they are able.
>
> Anyone who imagines that a cavalry regiment [in combat] can be controlled with the voice or the trumpet at a whim, as if on a peacetime manoeuvre, has never been in such a close combat in which all arms are involved.

Meerheim continues with his account of the struggle for Semenovskaya:

> Then the Saxon Cuirassier brigade was charged by Russian dragoons; these were at once overthrown but, in the heat of the moment, a group of our officers and men had gone too far in the chase. They were surrounded and mostly cut down by the enemy cavalry, including Colonel von Leysser. *Premierleutnant* Scheffel was wounded; ridden over and captured. His story is of interest.
>
> A Russian cuirassier was escorting this wounded officer prisoner (who had already been plundered) to the rear, 'steering' him by means of blows with the flat of his sword and urging him to greater speed with the occasional kick. Scheffel managed to pick up a sword lying by the roadside and stabbed the cuirassier in the mouth so that he fell off his horse, whereupon Scheffel escaped into a nearby small wood. Here he was found by some French *maraudeurs* who, in order not to have any witnesses to their actions, threw him out on to the meadow, where he collapsed unconscious. The cool evening air awoke him; as luck would have it, a group of survivors of his regiment, riding to their bivouac, rode close by and the wounded man managed to cry out, was found, and brought back to safety.

The Saxon and Westphalian cuirassiers were to be put further to the test later in the day, but the result of the battle in the centre was that the Russians were eventually forced to give up the ruins of Semenovskaya. Withdrawing sullenly, they formed a new line of battle some hundreds of paces to the east of it.

The allies were too exhausted to push on further.

13

The Southern Flank –
the Struggle for Utitsa

THE CHARACTER OF the combat in this sector of the field differed from that in the centre and the north. This was because of the nature of the terrain which, here, was swampy and heavily covered with scrub and low woods, including silver birch, hazel, and small pine trees. These factors limited mobility, visibility, and the effective use of artillery and cavalry. Here, it was mainly a close-range, infantry fire fight, with the artillery and cavalry in a secondary role.

Conrady, a Westphalian infantry officer, left us his account of the fighting here this day.

> Accompanied by an earth-shaking artillery bombardment, our various corps began to advance. First, Poniatowski's V Corps (which had the longest distance to cover) in the direction of Utitsa, then the divisions of Compans and Desaix who were to assault the great redoubts [*sic*] at Semenovskaya.
>
> At about seven o'clock, Ney's III Corps received orders to advance and our VIII Corps was to follow in support. I must explain that on this day our two Cuirassier regiments operated under command of Latour-Maubourg, our light cavalry under Murat, and the entire infantry under Ney. Thus Junot had effectively no command. He was most insulted but there was nothing that he could do about it.
>
> The infantry marched up in two lines behind the III Corps which was formed in columns. At the start of the battle the III Corps captured some of the redans [*sic*] in front of Semenovskaya; during Russian attempts to retake these works, the Westphalians advanced to the right of the III Corps and came under Ney's personal command.
>
> As the assaults of Poniatowski and Davout were failing at this time, the VIII Corps was ordered to advance to fill the gap between them on the right wing. The 1st Brigade, 23rd Division under General Damas was sent towards the enemy left wing to seize a small wood. During this advance, we were attacked several times by Russian cuirassier regiments. This delayed our advance because we had repeatedly to form square to drive them off. Our Westphalian artillery gave us good support during these attacks.
>
> The 23rd Division drove the enemy out of the wood and held it to provide communication with the Poles who were advancing on Utitsa

around it. General Ochs's 24th Division had remained in support behind the redans; it now advanced on to the plain. Lieutenant-Colonel von Rauschenplatt's 1st Light Battalion were leading and they were attacked by enemy cavalry; they received them with such an effective discharge of battalion fire that the Russians withdrew with heavy losses. General Ochs now advanced with the Westphalian Guard and occupied the plain.

At about 3 o'clock [during the final struggle for Semenovskaya], Ney received orders to break the Russian line in the forest south of Semenovskaya but the Russians called up reserves and a murderous fight developed in which their artillery caused especially heavy casualties to the VIII Corps. Ney ordered the Westphalian Jaeger Carabiniers (who were armed with rifles) to advance to very close to the Russian batteries and to kill the gun crews.

The Russians repeated their cavalry attacks which were again repelled. The 2nd Brigade, under General von Borstell, advanced in column of attack against the enemy line and forced it back to a small wood in which was a Russian battery and many of their Jaegers and these caused the Westphalians many more casualties. Ney ordered General Ochs to storm this wood. As all the generals of the 23rd Division (who were closest to the wood) were already dead or wounded, Ochs requested permission to leave his 24th Division to take command of the assault; Ney granted it.

Ochs took command of the 1st Brigade, 23rd Division, took the lead together with Lieutenant-Colonel Jungkurt of the 6th Line Regiment, led the brigade into the wood and cleared it. The rest of the Westphalian corps followed. Having lost this vital feature, the Russian left wing withdrew.

This last attack, which took place at about 5 o'clock, cost us many casualties but was decisive.

Private Fleck, of the Westphalian Garde-Jaeger Battalion, gave a less-dry account of the start of this momentous day:

We Jaegers stood on the flank of the army. Since sunrise the cannon had thundered and we had lost quite a lot of men. We stood immobile as we waited to be mustered by the Emperor. Finally he appeared with a large and glittering following. He dismounted; we presented arms and moved into open order. He passed along, inspecting every man and every so often he paused to inspect a rifle. During this time we were still under artillery fire but he seemed not to notice even though about thirty of our battalion fell.

On the right wing of my company a howitzer shell burst and took off one arm each from two Jaegers standing in the first rank and ripped out the belly of another in the second rank. In spite of having seen all this, the Emperor quietly continued with his muster. After he had finished, we marched off to the front.

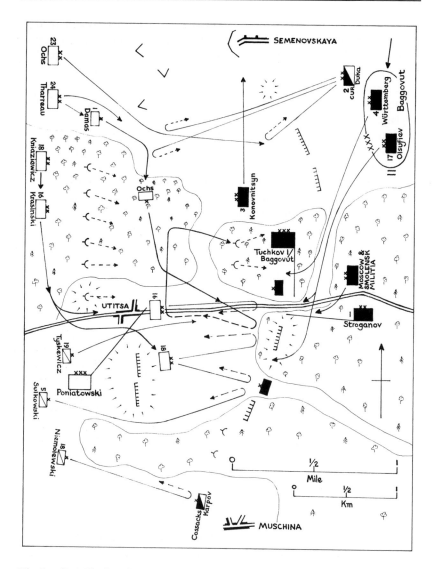

The Southern Flank: Utitsa

Conrady also tells us how difficult it was for the generals to oversee and control the battle in this sector of the field, as the troops frequently fought in small, practically independent groups within the forest, increasingly isolated and without any knowledge of what was happening on other parts of the field. Friend often fired upon friend and the confusion was complete.

The Westphalian Jaegers who, as already said, had, on Ney's express orders, to close up to the enemy's artillery batteries, suffered particularly heavy casualties. Fleck tells us that one discharge of canister from the flank killed thirty-five men of his battalion and as many again were wounded.

Later in the day, the Jaegers were mistaken for Russians (because of their dark-green uniforms) by their own Light Infantry Battalion, and were fired upon. Happily, only a few men were hit on this occasion.

Fleck's Garde-Jaeger Battalion started the day of this battle 550 strong; that evening their strength had dropped to between twenty and thirty present and fit for duty! Conrady's regiment lost nine officers and 397 men. Linsingen's battalion started the day with 700 men on parade; they lost ten officers and 341 men during the day.

Our young Westphalian infantry captain, Morgenstern, left us this version of events which took place just after the fatal wounding of General Tharreau.

The Adjutant-Major brought me the order to leave my company to take over the grenadier company whose captain, von Hugo, and *premier leutnant*, von Poblotzky, had been badly wounded. I left my company and went to the grenadiers where the battalion commander introduced me as their acting commander. At the edge of the wood we halted. General Damas sent in the four Voltigeur companies of the brigade to reconnoitre the situation and to make contact with the V Corps. Shortly afterwards, we heard our Voltigeurs in a lively engagement with the enemy. The firing increased and the commander of the Voltigeurs, Lieutenant-Colonel Wetzel, called for support. It was sent in the form of volunteers from the centre companies. . . . We succeeded in driving the enemy out of this area of the woods.

During this violent combat we lost our popular brigade commander, General Damas, killed by a musket ball. His place was taken by Colonel von Füllgraf.

At the far edge of the wood, which stretched in a wide concave arc to each side of us, we saw a gently sloping hill on which was a battery of artillery (drawn by an all-grey team) behind which masses of infantry lay on the ground. [This is one of the only two references that I have been able to find of Russian troops making use of cover in this battle.]

In front of the guns — and also lying on the sloping ground — was the line of skirmishers which we had just driven out of the wood. As soon as the Russian artillery saw us we were greeted with salvoes of effective fire.

We withdrew some hundreds of paces into the wood, leaving a chain of Voltigeurs at its edge, under cover of the trees and bushes. Nevertheless, the battery continued to plague us with shot and shell, causing numerous casualties, mostly due to splinters from the trees.

At last, up came Colonel von Füllgraf. In his sonorous voice he commanded: 'Let us be brave, Comrades. At the double! Shoulder arms! March!'

His words had an electric effect upon us. With a great 'Hooray!', the brigade burst out of the wood, the 2nd Regiment leading. Our fine regimental band boosted our courage and confidence until at last our drummers, beating out the monotonous '*pas de charge*', drove us at a rapid pace against the enemy.

The round shot of the Russian battery caused havoc in our ranks and at any moment we must expect a volley of canister from them. Our total destruction was ensured, however, by the mass of enemy infantry, whose full strength we had not at first appreciated, but which we could now see much exceeded our own. There was no sign of any support forthcoming from our side for our more-than-bold charge. Our Hurrahs died out in the face of the superior Russian infantry formation; our paces became shorter and shorter; the only noises from our side were the encouraging shouts of our officers from in front of our ranks.

Füllgraf now recognised the hopelessness of his undertaking. He ordered a withdrawal. Another hundred paces and we would have experienced the shame of being thrown back in disarray.

Thanks to the efforts of all our officers and NCOs, we managed to reach the protection of the woods in relatively good formation if with heavy loss. There we were met by the colonel of a Polish regiment which had just come up; he saluted us respectfully and suggested that '*les braves Westphalians*' should reform behind his regiment which would take over the defence of the edge of the wood.

We had extracted ourselves from a difficult situation with honour, but it took all the efforts of the officers to rectify the bad impression left by our commander, who had been so foolhardy as to assault a well-placed battery, supported by a strong infantry force, with three very weak, unsupported battalions.

After a while, Colonel von Füllgraf received an order to leave the woods in the hands of the Poles and to join that part of our corps under General Ochs. We marched off to the left and soon found the detached battalion of the 6th Regiment with which was General Ochs. He directed the now-reunited brigade to a clear part of the forest. . . . Soon, we saw through the trees, the glitter of the sun on the weapons of a force of advancing Russians. Their skirmishers began to fire at us; our Voltigeurs advanced rapidly to counteract them. Suddenly, from the right wing, there was a mighty battle cry. A strong Russian infantry line was charging at our 6th Regiment. One shout from General Ochs was enough to bring the well-drilled veterans of this fine regiment into disciplined silence. At a range of twenty paces at the most they received the death-defying Russians with well-aimed battalion salvoes. Ochs then gave the order: 'Bayonets at the ready! Double march!' and led the 6th against the enemy who fled in wild panic. Our regiment followed, and on our advance we met a second

General Charles Kniaziewicz, commander, 18th Infantry Division, V (Polish) Corps in 1812
At the Beresina crossing, Kniaziewicz took over command of the V Corps when both Poniatowski and Dombrowski were incapacitated, the former by sickness, the latter with wounds.
By kind permission of the Polish Institute, London

Russian line which, however, contented itself with taking up their defeated comrades before withdrawing rapidly, leaving a strong line of skirmishers behind them.

These were wonderful moments! As if by magic they restored the lost confidence of our young soldiers!

This example, taken from life in the front line of a Napoleonic battle, demonstrates just how brittle – and fickle – a thing the combat morale of a body of soldiers may be.

What of the Poles of the V Corps who had spearheaded the advance on the southern flank? Malibran and Chelminski give us this account of their fortunes.

Poniatowski set off on his flanking march at 5 o'clock in two columns, one under Isidor Krasinski (who replaced General Zayonczek as commander,

16th Division when the latter was wounded at Smolensk), he was followed by the 18th Division under Kniaziewicz. The columns were surrounded by a large swarm of light troops to keep the Cossacks and Russian skirmishers at bay.

Utitsa was found to be occupied by some Russian Jaegers and militia with a battery of artillery but they were speedily ejected. Once the village had been taken, Poniatowski turned his attention to the next Russian position to his front. It so happened that the Russian commander in this sector, Tuchkov I, had already had to detach four line regiments of Konovnitzyn's 3rd Division of his III Corps north to help Prince Bagration's 2nd Army, which was being violently attacked by Ney and Davout. He thus now had only Count Stroganov's 1st Grenadier Division, the 20th and 21st Jaegers from the 3rd Division, the 49th and 50th Jaegers of the 27th Division (which were forced down into his sector by the fighting around the *flèches*), the militia and Karpov's 1500 Cossacks. The opposition to the Polish advance was thus considerably weaker than it might have been. When the Polish-Westphalian advance developed into a serious threat, however, Kutuzov sent the 17th Division of Baggovut's II Corps south to prop up his crumbling left wing and so restored the situation. The advance on the southern flank stagnated.

Lieutenant-General Baggovut, commander II Russian Corps, reported as follows on events in this sector:

> I was ordered by Your Excellency to take the 17th Division (four line infantry regiments) to go to the support of our left wing. I left the 4th Division behind. Somewhat to the left of our centre was Major-General Count Sievers's command, whose batteries were in action on the heights, but, because of the light calibre of their [horse artillery] guns could not inflict much damage on the enemy. I thus replaced them with Position Battery No. 17 (Colonel Dietrichs II) and detached the Infantry Regiment Ryazan as escort. I ordered the Infantry Regiment Brest to send skirmishers into the woods on the left-hand side of the battery. The enemy now assaulted Position Battery No. 17 with artillery and three columns of infantry, but our guns drove them back.
>
> Lieutenant-General Tuchkov I now told me that the enemy was advancing against the hill on the left wing. I sent the Infantry Regiments Belozersk and Willmanstrand with six guns of Position Battery No. 17 to help him. They were replaced in the centre by six light guns of Light Battery No. 33. Lieutenant-General Olsufjif [*sic*] commanded this force until it reached the left wing where Lieutenant-General Tuchkov I took it over and placed the six guns on the hill.
>
> Enemy artillery bombarded the hill and they sent forward a strong force of skirmishers. Our artillery drove them back. A second attack reached the foot of the hill; Tuchkov mounted a counter-attack bayonet charge with

one battalion of the Infantry Regiment Belozersk and the Grenadier Regiment Pawlof [*sic*]. The enemy were beaten back.

Tuchkov was now wounded; I took over command of the left wing.

The Duke of Württemberg now arrived with the Infantry Regiments Kremenchug and Minsk and I deployed them between our left wing ar d Count Sievers's command The artillery they brought with them w is deployed as follows: six guns of Position Battery No. 4 – to relieve the six guns of Position Battery No. 17 on the hill; those of Position Battery No. 17 and six of Position Battery No. 4 I sent to Sievers.

The enemy now tried to make an outflanking move to the south. I sent some of Karpov's Cossack regiments against them. The enemy launched a strong counter-attack against them even though their task had been merely one of reconnaissance.

The enemy now assaulted Major-General Count Ivelich's brigade; Ivelich advanced with four companies of the Infantry Regiment Brest, fired a volley and charged with the bayonet, but was beaten back by the fire of the artillery which accompanied the enemy column. Ivelich was wounded; Major-General Vadkovsky took over command in his place. I sent the Infantry Regiment Willmanstrand and 500 Moscow Militia to help him and ordered him to mount a counter-attack using the Infantry Regiment Ryazan as well.

The counter-attack succeeded but General Vadkovsky and Colonel Sokerev (Commanding Officer, Infantry Regiment Willmanstrand) were wounded. An enemy column now advanced between Vadkovsky and me. I sent one battalion of the Grenadier Regiment Taurien [*sic*] to stop them and sent Major-General Shakhovsky, with the Infantry Regiment Minsk, against them. The enemy were forced back. Colonel Krasavin (Commanding Officer, Infantry Regiment Minsk) was wounded.

The enemy now began another attempt to outflank us in the south, with infantry and cavalry against our guns on the hill. A counter-attack by Colonel Pyshnitskoi and the Infantry Regiment Kremenchug saved our guns with a bayonet charge.

Now I regrouped to the rear and withdrew the guns from the hill so as to come into line with the rest of our army. The enemy followed up; we reformed and stopped him but darkness stopped our further advance.

The Duke of Württemberg, commander of the Russian 4th Division this day, had been transferred from the north of the battlefield to the centre (as we have already seen in the mighty struggle for Semenovskaya) and left us his version of events around Utitsa.

The battle in the centre was in direct relationship with that on the southern flank (Poniatowski versus Tuchkov). The combat there started at Utitsa perhaps 30 minutes or an hour after the assault on the Bagration *flèches*. Poniatowski gradually won ground with the V Corps and was supported by the VIII Corps, which was to his north, towards Davout's I Corps.

When the 17th Division reached Tuchkov I's sector, he launched a counter-attack against the allies, who had in the meantime taken the hill east of Utitsa. The Poles were forced back to Utitsa. Tuchkov I was wounded in this action and Baggovut took over command in his place. Baggovut's troops now occupied a position quite in advance of the remnants of the 2nd Army (commanded after Bagration left the field first by Konovnitzyn then by Dokhturov) who had by now been pushed back east of Semenovskaya.

This, I think, describes the events that took place on the Russian left wing between 6 o'clock and midday. History will provide many interesting and credible details of the actions that took place here, but will not amend the sequence shown above.

The Duke's account of the events later in the day, after the crisis in the centre had passed, are also revealing.

Baggovut called repeatedly and urgently for his missing 4th Division to bolster up the Utitsa sector; his messages came fast and furiously. But the 4th Division could not move out of its hell [in the centre] unless it had express orders so to do from Barclay.

At last, Barclay told me to go down to the left wing with the Infantry Regiments Kremenchug and Minsk as soon as Ostermann's IV Corps had relieved me behind the 24th Division. At this point, my 1st Brigade was under heavy French cavalry attack and could not leave its post.

As I marched past the Moscow Militia, their commanders thought that we were retreating until I reassured them that we were on the way to reinforce Baggovut's II Corps. By this time, all the fighting had stopped. Poniatowski was sitting passively in his position behind Utitsa, and we were sitting passively around the much-disputed hill. Only the Jaegers of the 3rd Division and the Grenadier Regiments St Petersburg and Taurien [sic] were still skirmishing in the scrub on the flank of the Russian corps.

. . . After the fighting had died down (around the Raevsky Battery), there was another clash at Baggovut's advanced position. A Westphalian column had pushed forward through the woods into the gap between Baggovut's command and our centre. Baggovut doubted my opinion that they were enemy troops but sent Prince Shakovsk with his 4th Jaegers and the Infantry Regiment Minsk to investigate. Shakovsk advanced without due caution; was greeted with a salvo of canister and was repelled with loss.

Baggovut was now convinced of the danger of his exposed position and withdrew to the hill of Tsarevo, on to the left wing of our main line.

Konovnitzyn now rode up and suggested that Baggovut must resume his former position. Baggovut was furious, but burst out: 'Very well, I'll take a handful of grenadiers and retake the bloody thing!' I asked for – and received – permission to lead the new assault which cost the Infantry Regiments Kremenchug and Minsk some further hundreds of casualties. A Polish counter-attack threw us back on to Kern's brigade (previously Ivelich's) and I was lucky to escape with my life and to save the four guns that I had with me.

Bogdanovich's account of events on the southern flank are generally in line with that outlined above:

At 5 o'clock in the morning, Poniatowski's V Corps moved off, at the first cannon shot, to assault the Russian left wing. But the leading division (Krasinsky's) met with such difficult terrain in the woods that they did not reach the old Moscow–Smolensk road until about 8 o'clock. The V Corps took Utitsa but further progress was stopped by the 1st Grenadier Division. Tuchkov I now withdrew east to the burial mound [hillock] and took up a new position. North of the mound was the Life Grenadier Regiment and the Grenadier Regiment Count Arakcheev; behind it, in reserve, the Grenadier Regiment Pavlov. On the mound itself were four guns (Konovnitzyn says six) and south of it the Regiments Ekaterinoslav and St Petersburg. Between the last two were twelve guns. The Regiment Tauride was sent into the woods to the north with Prince Shakovsk's 4th Jaeger Regiment and the 49th and 50th Jaegers of Neverovsky's 27th Division who had been skirmishing for two hours with the I and V [*sic*, Bogdanovich must surely have meant the III] French Corps. Behind (Tuchkov I's) III Corps was the Moscow [and Smolensk] Militia.

As Poniatowski did not know of the detachment of Konovnitzyn's division north to Semenovskaya, he did not dare to advance further in case he became outflanked and cut off. It was only at 10.30, when the VIII (Westphalian) Corps came up on his left to support him, that Poniatowski set up a battery of forty guns and launched an assault to take the burial mound.

The assault succeeded and the 1st Grenadier Division was forced off the mound.

Tuchkov I withdrew a little. It was at this point that Lieutenant-General Alsufevev arrived at Tuchkov I's location with the Infantry Regiments Willmanstrand and Belozersk [17th Division, II Corps] to support the threatened Russian left wing. Tuchkov decided to counter-attack at once with fresh troops, and led the assault with the Pavlov Grenadier Regiment. Alsufevev's troops formed up on the right of the 1st Grenadier Division and thus outflanked the Polish left wing. At the same time, Count Stroganov, with the Grenadier Regiments St Petersburg and Ekaterinoslav (with the Life Grenadier Regiment and Grenadier Regiment Count Arakcheev in second line) made another outflanking advance on the Poles.

Poniatowski withdrew into Utitsa; the Russians retook the mound and set up a battery of six heavy guns on it. The action rested here on the southern flank for some time.

In the fighting Tuchkov I had been fatally wounded and Major-General Count Ivelich had been wounded. After six hours of combat, the Russians still held all their original ground except for the Bagration *flèches* and the Semenovskaya valley [and Borodino village].

As has been said, there was relative quiet on the southern flank for some hours although low-level skirmishing continued throughout. Bog-danovich continues:

> At about 4 o'clock, the VIII (Westphalian) Corps, led by General Ochs, advanced against Baggovut's right wing (Prince Shakovsk's 4th Jaegers and the Infantry Regiment Minsk). Baggovut withdrew about 1000 metres [1100 yd] and by 5 o'clock was in line with the rest of the Russian army. When Poniatowski saw this, he ordered the 13th (Polish) Hussars under Colonel Tulinski (and supported by the three other cavalry regiments of the V Corps) to outflank Baggovut's left wing. [Here, Bogdanovich's account of events at this point differs from that given by our eye-witness, the Duke of Württemberg, described above.]

The Duke of Württemberg was still on the mound with four guns and the Infantry Regiment Kremenchug (now reduced to only 300 men) but had to fall back in the face of this threat. Poniatowski occupied the mound. Some Russian generals present criticised Württemberg's with-drawal so, after a heated discussion, he took the Regiments Kremenchug and Minsk (only 500 men together) with four guns and mounted a counter-attack. The Regiments Ryazan and Brest followed in support. The Regiment Minsk charged the mound but were beaten back by a counter-charge by the 12th Polish Lancers.

This was the end of the action on the southern wing.

14

The Northern Flank – the Russian Raid

AT ABOUT 7.30 on the morning of the battle, Cossack patrols sent out by Ataman Platov (commander of the Don Cossack Pulks on the extreme northern Russian flank) discovered a ford across the lower Kolocha in the area of the hamlet of Seloe Novie. Seeing that the terrain west of the stream was empty of allied forces, Platov sent one of his aides, Colonel Prince Ernst von Hessen-Philippsthal (who was serving with the Russian army in a voluntary capacity) to Kutuzov's headquarters to ask permission to mount a raid into this vacuum to see what damage might be done to the enemy. On his way to Kutuzov at Gorki, the prince met the tireless and imaginative Colonel Toll of Kutuzov's staff. After discussing the projected raid, Toll undertook to recommend the idea to the Commander-in-Chief which he at once did. Toll suggested that, not just Platov's Cossacks, but also General Uvarov's I Cavalry Corps should be committed to the action. Kutuzov agreed, saying simply: '*Eh bien! Prenez le!*' [Very well! Take it!]

Fortune had favoured the spontaneous plan because it was at about this time that the hotly disputed Raevsky Battery had just been retaken from the Viceroy, Prince Eugène's IV Corps, and the Russian high command was already anxious about their ability to hold out in the centre. Such a diversion might ease the pressure on their centre, and it would make – they hoped – good use of the available forces on their right wing.

There has been considerable criticism of this raid for its failure to achieve more than it actually did on the day. This criticism is utterly misplaced, and is the result of repeated misinterpretations of the effects of the raid upon Napoleon's plan for the battle.

Borodino was to have been the 'Austerlitz of 1812', the crushing victory that Napoleon had been pursuing since he crossed the Russian border, the victory his frantic – and abortive – chase for which had ruined his cavalry, reduced his army to a fraction of its former strength, and drawn him deep into the gloomy wastes of this vast, desolate, and hostile country. This day was critical to his final success. If he could not destroy the enemy here today, if he failed to break their will to continue the war, he would have failed in his entire gigantic gamble. All would have been for nothing.

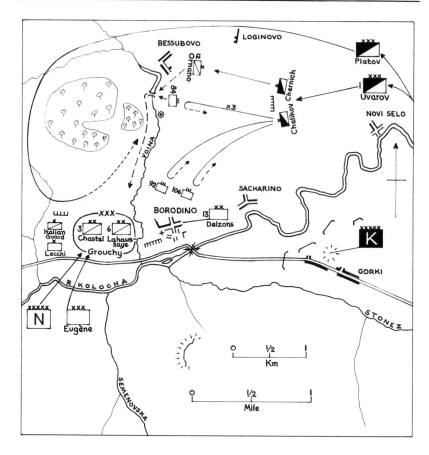

The Northern Flank: Uvarov's raid, 1200–1400 hours

As history records, all *was* for nothing.

Napoleon was acutely aware of the critical importance of time in warfare, the necessity never to waste a second if his schemes were to succeed. From him we have the following quotations that underline the importance he placed upon the subject: 'Ask of me anything but time!' 'Ground we may recover, time never!' 'I may lose ground but I will never lose a minute!'

To achieve his crushing victory, Napoleon's forces had to destroy the Russian army during the hours of daylight on 7 September. By the time darkness fell, the Russians had to be streaming away in total defeat, with the Emperor's victorious cavalry hacking the defenceless fugitives to pieces, and a throng of beaten enemy generals listening to his victorious cant as his hussars threw yet more captured colours and standards on to the heaps at his feet, and his ADCs tallied up the numbers of prisoners

The monument to Uvarov's raid
It was across this wide, open plain that Uvarov and Platov rode to spread panic among Prince Eugène's IV Corps.
Author's collection

and guns taken. This was why the assault was to begin at such an early hour.

If the Russians could hold out as an intact fighting force until dark, Napoleon would have failed. Anything that prevented his army from breaking their line this day, would work immensely in the Russians' favour.

It should also be remembered that the Russian raid was a completely *ad hoc* idea, not part of the prepared plan, and mounted only to take advantage of a lucky chance. There were no written orders, no targets were set, no agenda laid down, and, most importantly, the force sent contained only one battery of artillery and no infantry at all. Thus, its ability to be a serious threat was almost nil. At the best, it was a glorified Cossack raid, snooping around on the enemy's apparently open left flank to see if Lady Luck would throw any juicy morsels in their path. This raid was meant by Kutuzov, and understood by Uvarov, to be merely a feint.

But let us examine just what the raid did achieve. All sources agree that the raid caused such a panic on the French left wing that Prince Eugène abandoned his planned third assault on the Raevsky Battery at about 12 o'clock, pulled his forces out of the front line before the works, and withdrew them to the west and back over the Kolocha to confront this new threat. By the time that the Russians withdrew eastwards back into their own lines and Eugène could redeploy his forces for the assault on the Battery, two hours had passed.

His withdrawal of the IV Corps and other forces from the front line caused a gap that had to be hurriedly filled by other allied units, thus distracting them from their primary tasks and further easing the pressure on the battered Russian centre.

Napoleon had made his plan for the day but here we see these bungling, incompetent Russians stealing not just a few minutes from 'The Master'; they stole two complete hours: two hours in which the Russian high command could review existing plans and revise them if needed; two hours in which shattered Russian regiments could be reorganised or replaced in the line; two hours in which exhausted Russian infantry and artillery ammunition could be replenished; two hours in which Russian reserves could be redeployed to the most threatened section of the front; two hours (and more) in which Montbrun's II Cavalry Corps had to fill a gap in the French line, in close range of the Russian artillery in and around the Battery, and during which they suffered immense damage. And it was two hours' time lost that 'The Master' was never to recover.

The question must also be asked: Should Prince Eugène be blamed for snatching the crushing victory, which he so desperately needed, from his adoptive father's grasp? For there is no doubt that the Russian 2nd Army had been knocked to pieces in the prolonged and bitter fighting at the *flèches* and at Semenovskaya, and its morale had suffered a severe blow when Bagration had been wounded. Many of the 2nd Army's units were close to dissolution by 12 o'clock, and it was already the reserves of their V Corps (the Guard) and the heavy cavalry who were holding the ring for Kutuzov in this sector.

The sudden and unexpected lifting of the French assaults here, caused by the need for their forces to side-step to the north to fill the gap in the line caused by Eugène's withdrawal of his units in response to the sudden appearance of Platov and Uvarov at his flank and rear, gave the 2nd Army a vital respite. Further, should Platov, Uvarov, and Toll be posthumously enshrined in Russia's annals as the true – but yet unsung – heroes of Borodino, and architects of Napoleon's crushing defeat in Russia in 1812?

The forces involved were:

I Cavalry Corps (Lieutenant-General and General-Adjutant F. P. Uvarov).
Major-General Chalikov: Life Guard Hussars, Life Guard Ulans, Life Guard Dragoons.
Major-General Chernich: Nizhin Dragoons, Elisabetgrad Hussars, Horse Artillery Battery Nr. 5. Total: 20 squadrons; 12 guns; about 2500 men.
General of Cavalry and Ataman Platov.
The Cossack Pulks of Ilovaisk V, Grekov XVIII, Khartonov VII, Denisov VII, Zhirov, Vlasov III, the Simferopol Tartar Regiment, and part of the Ataman's Cossack Pulk. Total about 5500 men.

Bogdanovich gives a slightly different Russian order of battle for this raid: 'Uvarov's command was: Life Guard Hussars, Life Guard Ulans, Life Guard Dragoons, Life Guard Cossacks, Ryazin Dragoons, Elisabetgrad Hussars and Horse Artillery Battery Nr. 2'. The composition of Platov's Cossacks is the same. As there was no dragoon regiment in the Russian army at this time with the title 'Ryazin', this must be a misprint for 'Nieschin' [Nizhin] and is confirmed by the orders of battle. Some eye-witness accounts speak of seeing 'yellow-clad Russian hussars' taking part in this raid. Two regiments wore yellow dolmans at this point: Ssum and Elisabetgrad but the Ssum regiment had light-blue pelisses whereas the Elisabetgrad regiment wore yellow. Thus, it is most likely that the Elisabetgrad regiment was actually part of this raiding force. Which artillery battery took part remains unresolved.

The force concentrated and moved off, crossing at the ford and debouching into the flat, open area north of Borodino. Here they split into two parts; Uvarov's Corps swinging to the south-west and south, Platov's Cossacks initially riding due west, crossing the upper Voina stream into a large expanse of scrub and bush, and then to turn south to lunge down at the Kolocha in the area of the hamlets of Valueva and Aleksinki, and thus threatening the rear of the Viceroy Eugène's IV Corps, his ammunition train, the wounded of the action so far, and the Kolocha bridging site, but — more importantly — aiming directly at Napoleon's command post at the Shevardino Redoubt!

The two groups were now separated by about 1500 metres (1640 yd), thus rendering mutually supportive action difficult if not impossible; each was playing his own game.

Meanwhile, just after midday, Prince Eugène had received orders from Imperial Headquarters to undertake another assault on the Raevsky Battery. Part of the Young Guard and the Reserve Cavalry were to support him.

General Sorbier had by now noticed that the Russian centre had been reinforced by the Duke of Württemberg's 4th Division and Ostermann's IV Corps. He assumed that a Russian counter-attack was imminent and took action to frustrate it. He brought up thirty-six guns from the Guards Artillery Park and a further forty-nine horse artillery pieces from Nansouty's and Latour-Maubourg's Reserve Cavalry Corps. These guns, and the IV Corps' own artillery, now opened up against Württemberg and Ostermann creating the 'hell' of crossfire so fittingly described earlier.

When Napoleon judged the Russian centre to have been pounded sufficiently to make an assault profitable, he sent orders for Eugène to launch his third attack on the Raevsky Battery. Just at this very moment, however, panic broke out in the rear of Eugène's IV Corps; Uvarov and

Platov had been sighted bearing down on their sparsely protected left flank. The train and baggage personnel near Aleksinki already knew enough about what Cossacks could do to their sorts if given the chance, and most fled to the rear at speed. Alarming reports spread in all directions, and more reached Eugène from Delzon and Ornano on his immediate left flank; the imminent assault on the Battery was abandoned in favour of more urgent damage control and the assurance of the survival of the IV Corps.

On the site of this action stands today a red sandstone monument to the I Cavalry Corps in commemoration of what went on here in September 1812. Engraved on the monument is a tactical map showing the Russian version of what happened. Just south of Bessubovo was a small lake formed by damming the Voina stream as it flowed south to join the Kolocha west of Borodino. Below the dam was a watermill. Because of its deep-cut nature south of the dam, and the lake above it, the only crossing point for some distance in either direction was the track over the dam itself. At the approach of Uvarov's cavalry, the available French forces in this sector were deployed as follows: Ornano's 12th Light Cavalry Brigade (9e and 19e *Chasseurs à Cheval*) just east of Bessubovo; 84e *Ligne* (in square) – east of the mill; 92e and 106e *Ligne* (also in square) – just north of Borodino. The 8e *Légère* is not shown and was probably in Borodino itself.

West of the Voina are shown (from east to west): La Haussaye's 6th Heavy Cavalry Division (7e, 23e, 28e, 30e Dragoons); Chastel's 3rd Light Cavalry Division (only the 6e, 8e, and 25e *Chasseurs à Cheval* are shown); the Italian Guard with artillery arrayed in front (apparently four cavalry regiments – Dragons de la Reine, Guard Dragoons, and possibly the 2nd and 3rd Italian *Chasseurs à Cheval*, although two of these 'cavalry' regiments might represent the two regiments of the Italian Guard Infantry that also seem to have been present here).

Colonel von Clausewitz was with Uvarov in his capacity as Chief-of-Staff, I Cavalry Corps; he suggested softening up the three French infantry squares with artillery fire but Uvarov rejected this as a waste of time. The Life Guard Hussars charged the steady 84e three times and were beaten off with loss each time. At last, Uvarov ordered the Russian horse artillery to unlimber. By this time, the 84e had withdrawn over the mill dam, but had to leave behind their two regimental artillery pieces.

Further Russian charges against the squares of the 92e and 106e were also fruitless. The total lack of an infantry component in the Russian force, and their very weak artillery support ruled out any serious action against Eugène's IV Corps which was now concentrated and ready to oppose their advance across the mill dam. The weak Russian bolt was shot.

Meanwhile, Platov had crossed the Voina at a ford above Bessubovo and was well west of Eugène's IV Corps, spreading panic in the rear echelons. When Napoleon was informed of this unexpected Russian thrust, he was ripped out of the torpor in which he had spent much of the day. As he himself had said; 'A good general may be beaten, but he should never be surprised'. He ordered the assaults on the Raevsky Battery and Semenovskaya to be called off (here he was a little late as Eugène had already done this) and for urgent action to be taken to secure the left flank. Roguet's division of the Young Guard was ordered north up the Kamenka stream to the Kolocha, and the Vistula Legion was brought forward to the Kamenka. Napoleon himself rode up to the new Moscow road and stayed there until it became obvious that Platov and Uvarov could achieve nothing.

After about two hours, Barclay sent orders to the two commanders to withdraw as it appeared that nothing was now being gained. Clearly, the Russian high command did not appreciate the breathing space that had just been won or the confusion that had been caused in the enemy's ranks. At about 4 o'clock, Platov and Uvarov moved off to return to Gorki.

When Uvarov reported to Kutuzov on the outcome of the action, the perception in Russian headquarters of events was such that Kutuzov replied: 'I know. May God forgive you!'

Eugène and the bulk of his forces had returned to the south bank of the Kolocha some two hours before and were now preparing for the final assault on the Battery.

15

The Final Assault on
the Raevsky Battery

AT ABOUT MIDDAY, the IV Cavalry Corps was ordered to take post between
the captured village of Semenovskaya and the Raevsky Battery. This was
to plug the gap in the French line, caused by the withdrawal of Prince
Eugène's IV Corps to the west, and to respond to the appearance of Platov
and Uvarov on his exposed left flank. Here they were subjected for some
hours to effective shot and shell from the Russian batteries in and around
the famous earthwork. The site on which General Lorge's 7th Cavalry
Division was placed (east of the junction of the Semenovka and Kamenka
streams) is in full view of the guns on this ridge, and only some 600 metres
(650 yd) away from them; the order to put them there caused a totally
needless waste of lives. [It is baffling that no commander dared to point
this out and have them moved into cover.] Roth von Schreckenstein (a
junior officer in the Saxon Zastrow Cuirassiers in the battle) gives us some
idea of the desperate situation in which these regiments found themselves:
'As men and horses were being shot all the time, the men were fully
occupied closing to the centre and telling off in their new files of three;
this constant telling off never stopped'.

Latour-Maubourg saw that, if he could move his corps somewhat to
the left, they would benefit from the cover afforded by a gentle dip in
the ground. He was loath to have his command carry out a full flank
march to the new site in case the Russians should seize the opportunity
to attack them as they did so. He thus sent repeated orders to his
subordinates, by means of his ADCs, to carry out several minor 'shuffles'
to achieve the same objective. Not having his commander's aims
explained to him, General Thielemann became increasingly frustrated by
the repeated visitations of his minions with apparently pointless instructions, and eventually, he boiled over.

Just as this happened, it was the bad luck of one of Latour-Maubourg's
adjutants, a Pole, to come to General Thielemann's Brigade to deliver
the next order for it to move to the left. He arrived just as Thielemann
was between the Gardes du Corps and the Zastrow Cuirassiers
exchanging his wounded horse for a new mount. Not seeing the general,
he delivered the order directly to the regimental commanders. Much to
Thielemann's surprise, his brigade began to move off, apparently of its

own accord. Spotting the adjutant, Thielemann rode up and demanded to know why the order had not been delivered to him. The hapless adjutant replied that Thielemann 'had not been at his post'. This was the last straw for the general. Flying into a rage, he drew his sabre and charged straight at the Pole, chasing him all the way back to Latour-Maubourg. Here, he explained to his astounded commander that he was not one of those who would allow himself to be ordered about by adjutants, much less be insulted by them. Furthermore, if the said adjutant showed his face anywhere near him again, he would run him through!

It says much for Latour-Maubourg's regard for Thielemann's proven reputation as a brave and competent commander, that he did not at once arrest him but calmed him down and took the trouble to explain his aims to him in detail.

Montbrun's II Cavalry Corps was subjected to a similar ordeal when it advanced into line north of Lorge's Division, just west of the Semenovka stream. The general himself was mortally wounded by a shell splinter as he rode at a walk along the front of his regiments. 'Good shot!' a Prussian trooper heard him murmur as he slid from his horse. Montbrun died at 5 o'clock that evening from the effects of his stomach wound; among the Germans in the *Grande Armée*, he was regarded as being one of the most honourable men in the French army.

Among Montbrun's regiments was the 1st Prussian Ulans, commanded by Major von Werder. At one point, von Werder's horse collapsed on top of him, killed by an artillery shot. When his men came to drag him out, they found him still with his pipe in his mouth! A shell exploded between the legs of General Subervie (commander, 16th Light Cavalry Brigade) but left him completely unhurt while two Prussian Ulans beside him (Arnold and Galopy by name) each lost a foot, ripped off by the same cannonball.

The same fate befell the Bavarian and Saxon cavalry in the 17th Light Cavalry Brigade of Chastel's 3rd Light Cavalry Division, Grouchy's III Cavalry Corps. After they had supported Eugène's second, successful, assault on the Raevsky Battery [the Russians rapidly retook the work], they were forced to stand from 10.00 in the morning to 3.00 in the afternoon in the angle east of the confluence of the Semenovka and Kolocha streams, enduring the close-range fire of the Russian artillery ranged along the northern end of that slight ridge. Caught like rats in a trap, the Saxon Prinz Albert Chevaux-légèrs lost over half their strength in dead and wounded in this time to no purpose at all.

It was only when Prince Eugène made his third (delayed) assault on the Battery, that this brigade was released from its senseless torture, just to be ripped to pieces by volleys of canister as they breasted the ridge north of the work and received fire from another Russian battery on the next ridge south of Gorki.

When Prince Eugène's troops returned to their position in front of the Battery, they prepared to make the third assault. This time, the infantry were to aim for the north flank of the structure; Montbrun's II Cavalry Corps was also to assault the northern side of it but to strike before the infantry arrived, and the IV Cavalry Corps was to swing around into it from the south.

As Roth von Schreckenstein wrote:

> General Auguste de Caulaincourt (one of Napoleon's ADCs and brother to the French ex-ambassador to the Tsar) was by now attached to the II Cavalry Corps but only in the capacity of a brigade commander, not at divisional or even corps level as some writers have suggested in the past. This error has been compounded by the King of Naples, who wrote in his Report (as he related the capture of the heights of Semenovskaya by Latour-Maubourg between 10.30 and 11.30): '*Je fis alors passer le Général Caulaincourt à la tête du 2. Corps de réserve; à peine fut il de l'autre côte du ravin, que je lui donné l'ordre, de charger sur la gauche tout ce qui se trouvé d'ennemis et de tâcher d'aborder la grande redoubte (Raevsky Battery) qui, nous prenant en flanc, nous faisait beaucoup de mal, s'il trouvait l'occasion favorable. Cet ordre fut executé avec autant de célérité que de bravoure.*'
>
> This '*occasion favorable*' did not occur until much later, after 2 o'clock, when Prince Eugène made his final assault on the Battery, probably at the same time as Thielemann received his orders for the same attack. At that point, however, the King of Naples was close to the village of Semenovskaya and a long way away from the II Cavalry Corps.
>
> By saying that Caulaincourt was 'at the head' of the II Cavalry Corps, Murat gives the distinct impression that he was actually in command of it. Chambray, on the other hand, has Caulaincourt (Blesson, page 180) at the head of Wathier's division after this general had been wounded.

The assault was preceded by a barrage of shot and shell from the 170 French and allied guns that were so arranged as to bring very effective cross-fire to bear on their target. The loss, earlier in the day, of the commander of the Russian Reserve Artillery, General Count Kutaisov, had meant that the great majority of the 300 guns remained idle throughout the battle, and the answering artillery fire was relatively ineffective.

By now, the ramparts of the Battery had been pounded into a shapeless mass, much of which had fallen into the ditch. The allied gunfire was so effective that Colonel Nikitin's battery of horse artillery, which was in action next to the Battery, lost ninety-three men and 113 horses in less than an hour. All eight of the reserve horse artillery batteries in this sector of the front were fully employed countering the allied barrage.

Defence of the Battery was now the responsibility of the gun crews themselves and the VI Russian Corps of General Dokhturov. It consisted of General Likhachev's 24th Division (seven battalions), who were deployed directly behind it in the valley of the Goruzka stream, with Kaptsevich's 7th Division to the north. The remnants of the IV and VII Russian Corps were slightly further to the east, on the next ridge, with the II and III Russian Cavalry Corps behind them. Those allied artillery projectiles which missed targets in the front Russian lines, found many a billet in these exposed reserve formations. It had been the aim that General Raevsky's VII Corps was to reorganise behind the reserve cavalry and then advance into line again south of the 24th Division. Despite all Paskevich's efforts, however, it was not until nightfall that the 26th Division could be brought forward again.

It was just before 3 o'clock when Eugène's third assault was finally mounted. The infantry divisions of Morand (1st) and Gérard (3rd) formed the first line (Gérard's on the right), with Domanget's 17th Light Cavalry Brigade on the left wing, up against the Kolocha. In the second line were Lecchi's Italian Guard (on the right) and Broussier's 14th Division with La Haussaye's 6th Cuirassier Division on the left. Claparède's Vistula Legion had advanced up from Shevardino to take post on the right of Lecchi's division.

The posting of the cavalry on the left wing was, of course, in line with classic military teaching; in this situation, however, it may have been more appropriate to make an exception to the rule. Bearing in mind that the cavalry was hemmed in on their left by the Kolocha, which was here a definite obstacle as it ran through its deeply cut channel, the chances for their successful deployment were virtually none. They could equally well have been deployed behind the infantry and would still have been available to exploit any tactical opportunities that might have arisen in the course of the action.

South of Gérard's division was Sebastiani's II Cavalry Corps, then Latour-Maubourg's IV Cavalry Corps.

Shortly after 12 o'clock, Kutuzov sent orders to General Tolstoy's IV Corps to retake Semenovskaya; despite all the efforts, bravery, and grim determination of the Russians, their attacks failed. Tolstoy was wounded in the process.

Meanwhile, Lorge's 7th Cuirassier Division was suffering the continued effects of the Russian artillery bombardment with great stoicism. In fact, now that they had moved a little further to the left, into a slight dip in the ground, their casualty rate had decreased somewhat. This relief was

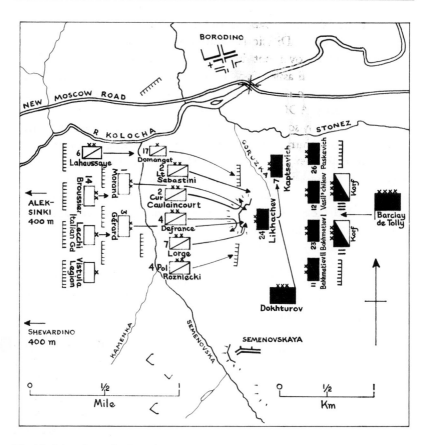

The Final Assault on the Raevsky Battery, 1500 hours

amplified by the fact that many of the shells which landed among them now had had their fuses set too long. Instead of bursting in the air just above their target to create maximum havoc, most buried themselves in the ground, the fuses were snuffed out, and the shells did not explode. The situation became so relaxed that General Thielemann ordered the men to break out their weeks-old rations of hard-tack biscuits and take a frugal snack.

Just before 3 o'clock, Eugène's infantry moved off to the assault. Shortly afterwards, one of Napoleon's ADCs galloped up to the impatient Thielemann and delivered to him the long-awaited message: 'On behalf of the Emperor, I bring you the order to attack!'

This same order had also been delivered to the II Cavalry Corps. Caulaincourt led Wathier's 2nd Cuirassier Division forward against the north flank of the Battery; Sebastiani's 2nd Light Cavalry and Defrance's

4th Cuirassier Divisions advanced directly on the front of the work, while Lorge's 7th Cuirassier Division advanced on its southern flank.

Barclay saw the movements in the enemy ranks opposite him and sent orders for the 1st Cuirassier Division to advance from its position behind the Lifeguard Division to counter the attack. Imagine his astonishment and rage when his ADC reported that the division was no longer there but had been sent by someone to the far southern wing earlier in the day!

That such an arbitrary move could have been carried out without Barclay having been consulted or informed speaks volumes on the practices in the Russian General Staff. As Barclay said:

> When I saw that the enemy were about to launch a violent assault, I at once sent for the 1st Cuirassier Division, supposing it to be still in the position which I had assigned to it, for I intended to keep it for a decisive blow. Unfortunately, someone – I don't know who – had moved it to the extreme left flank. All my adjutant could do was to collect just the two regiments of Lifeguard Cuirassiers and bring them to me by companies as quickly as he could.

By the time these two regiments had assembled, the three enemy corps were well into their advance and it was clear to Barclay that it would be suicide to commit them against such odds. What actually happened in this massive allied cavalry assault has been obscured by dubious, partisan French reports, generated at Napoleon's instigation and swallowed whole by generations of his adoring fans ever since. Which regiment was it that was first into the Battery? Which regiment actually took – and held – it?

As we shall see, Napoleon's official 'Rumour Mill' worked at top speed and with its customary efficiency to ensure that posterity would be forced to accept *his* version of events. In the years following the battle, however, still, small voices could be heard – by those willing to listen – that must lead us to treat this Napoleonic Bulletin with the circumspection now accorded to so much else that he wrote, or commanded to be written.

Meerheim described the final assault on the Raevsky Battery as follows:

> The redoubt lay at the top of a steep slope rather like the one that we had had to climb to get into Semenovskaya. [This I cannot understand; the slope from the west up to the site of the Redoubt is level and gentle.] It was covered by a fairly wide ditch but built, happily, only of loose earth, without palisades and obviously constructed in a hurry.
>
> On the side facing us there was a deep, narrow valley [Not today!] like a second ditch that we also had to cross before we could storm the actual crest of the ridge. In the Battery itself were perhaps twelve or more guns; the remaining space was filled with infantry. The ditch and the 'ravine'

were also filled with infantry. Behind the Battery were several fairly strong squares of infantry relatively close together and ranged along the far side of the valley east of the ridge on which the Battery stood. We saw (or rather felt) the presence of a strong force of artillery also on that ridge. Apart from this, we could see several lines of infantry and cavalry in reserve further back. In the dip towards Borodino [along the Goruzka stream] were more masses of infantry and cavalry which had previously been concealed from our view.

We charged at the 'ravine' and ditch, the horses clearing the bristling fences of bayonets as they would have *Chevaux de frise*. The combat was frightful! Men and horses hit by gunshots collapsed into the ditches and thrashed around among the dead and dying, each trying to kill the enemy with their weapons, their bare hands, or even their teeth. To add to this horror, the succeeding ranks of assaulting cavalry trampled over the writhing mass as they drove on to their next targets – the infantry squares – who greeted them with well-aimed volleys. [Von Meerheim now speaks of Russian infantry in huts in the valley east of the Battery firing out of the windows at them but I can find no trace of a similar account of such constructions, and the nearest village east of the Battery is Kniaskovo, over 1600 metres (1750 yd) away.]

Despite all the perils and obstacles, we were unstoppable and burst over and into the Battery, inspired by the examples of our commanders, Generals Latour, Thielemann, and our brigade adjutant von Minkwitz. The interior of the Battery was an indescribable mess of infantry and cavalry all intent on killing one another. The garrison of the place fought to the last.

Napoleon (and many historians since) attributed the final capture of Raevsky's Battery to French cuirassiers under the leadership of Caulaincourt. This, on-the-spot, eye-witness account, together with the carefully conducted investigation of Roth von Schreckenstein in his book *Die Kavallerie in der Schlacht an der Moskva*, should finally lay this ghost.

Von Schreckenstein wrote:

If I return again to the Report of the King of Naples of 9 September concerning the participation of the Reserve Cavalry in the battle, it is because this report contains a number of inaccuracies that have been repeated in subsequent documents including the Bulletin by the Marquis de Chambray of 10 September. In my footnote 30 to section 10 I have already shown how completely wrongly Chambray describes Latour-Maubourg's attack on Semenovskaya village. Chambray is equally unclear on page 180 concerning the capture of the Raevsky Battery where he has Caulaincourt enter the work by wheeling to the left, having previously charged a line of the enemy.

This is what he wrote: 'Eugène ordered the divisions of Broussier,

Morand, and Gérard to cease firing and to storm [the Battery]. At the same time, Caulaincourt, at the head of Wathier's (Cuirassier) division, overthrew the line of the enemy that was opposite to him, then, wheeling left, charged through the troops close behind the redoubt then, turning back towards the work, entered it from the rear. Eugène stormed over the parapet from the front at this same instant; all who defended themselves were cut down. Twenty-one guns fell into French hands. Wathier resumed his position on Eugène's right flank. Caulaincourt had been fatally wounded in the redoubt itself. It was now 3 o'clock. . .'

According to this, it seems that the Marquis de Chambray was ignorant of the fact that it was only Defrance's division that assaulted on the right of the redoubt and that Wathier's division attacked it from the direction of Borodino [that is, from the northern side], while the Saxon cavalry penetrated into it from the direction of Semenovskaya [the south]. This writer [Chambray] relates nothing of the active participation of Latour-Maubourg's (IV) corps here because there was nothing about it in the Bulletin and nothing in the Report.

I feel that it is quite possible that Caulaincourt was wounded near the Battery, but I feel that it is quite unacceptable for the King of Naples to bury the victor's laurels with *him*.

I further dispute the claim that he overthrew a line of enemy infantry behind the redoubt. It is incredible that the King of Naples seems to have forgotten that Montbrun was in command of all the II Cavalry Corps at the redoubt and that he was so close to the Battery two hours before the final storm that he lost his life.

It is also astounding that the King brings the capture of the heights of Semenovskaya (which was completed by 12 o'clock) directly into context with the final assault on the Raevsky Battery which, as is well known, took place at about 3 o'clock. It is as if the impression is meant to be given that nothing happened on the battlefield for three hours; that Latour-Maubourg was completely inactive. Or perhaps sections of the King's Report were removed at Napoleon's instructions to glorify Caulaincourt.

Latour-Maubourg was the senior allied cavalry commander in the vicinity of the Battery [at the time of its capture]; the charge into the Battery was only the preliminary to its final capture which was utterly dependent upon the defeat of the Russian infantry arraigned behind it. There is no doubt that it was Latour-Maubourg's cavalry corps, supported by Defrance's division (the Carabiniers etc.) that carried out this difficult task. I am in a position to confirm that he gave all the orders on the right-hand side of the Battery and that a considerable time elapsed before the Viceroy's infantry came up.

According to an eye-witness who related the following to us the next morning, Napoleon was standing by Berthier (at Shevardino) when the latter, squinting through his telescope, said 'The redoubt is taken, the Saxon cuirassiers are in it!'

Napoleon took the telescope, peered through it and said: 'You are wrong, they are dressed in blue; they are my cuirassiers'.

What Napoleon *may* have seen through his telescope, from his distant vantage point at Shevardino through all the smoke and confusion, was the 14th Polish Cuirassier Regiment which at this point formed the third rank of Thielemann's Saxon brigade as it followed the two Saxon regiments into the Battery. The uniform of the Polish cuirassiers was almost identical to that of their French comrades. Or they may have been the Westphalian Cuirassiers (of Lepel's brigade, 7th Division) who followed us.

In any case, Napoleon's regard for the truth was such that he would have said that which he wished to have posterity believe, knowing full well that none of those present would have dared to contradict him.

Roth von Schreckenstein continues: 'One thing is certain, in his 18th Bulletin, Napoleon attributed the capture of the Battery to Caulaincourt and mentioned the IV Cavalry Corps only in connection with the capture of Semenovskaya. Latour-Maubourg was extremely angry at this misinterpretation of the true events.'

As von Schreckenstein stated, the capture of the Battery itself was nothing without the defeat of all the Russian infantry in the valley of the Goruzka stream directly behind it.

All eye-witness accounts of the final storming of the Battery speak of being surprised at the presence of strong Russian infantry forces 'concealed in the steep-sided ravine' directly to the east of the work. The heat of battle may have distorted individual memories of the sequence of events, their timing, and of the terrain on which they occurred, but it is inexplicable that so many should agree that there was such a well-defined geographical feature there. There is a valley, it is true, but it is only marginally more steeply sloped than the western side of the ridge on which the Battery is built. The valley does, however, offer excellent cover from enemy view and fire (except artillery shells). As to how far this may be interpreted as an intentional use of the terrain by the Russians to conceal and protect their forces must remain up to the reader to judge; at least no Russian commander claims credit for having used the ground for this purpose, and several bewail the fact that it was not done, thus contributing to the very heavy casualties that they suffered this day.

Whoever was first into the Battery in this final assault, it is clear that the cavalry reached it before Eugène's infantry did, and that the II, III, and IV Cavalry Corps were all involved. The cavalry, of course, could *take* the ground, but it requires infantry (now as then) to *hold* it for any length of time.

When the massed allied cavalry rolled forward to assault the insignificant, battered earthwork, the infantry flanking it on the crest of the ridge formed square as the command, 'Prepare to receive cavalry!' rang out. This meant, of course, that the allied artillery, firing as they were over the heads of their own cavalry, could cause much more havoc in the densely packed Russian regiments than when they were in three-deep line.

Bogdanovich describes the final charge as follows:

Wathier's division crossed the Semenovka stream at the mouth of the Kamenka; passed left of the Raevsky Redoubt and hit part of the VI Corps in the Goruzka valley. The 5th Cuirassiers turned right and went over the ditch and rampart into the redoubt but were forced out again by infantry fire. Caulaincourt was fatally wounded by a musket ball to the throat.

General Bakhmetiev I (commander, 23rd [*sic*] Division) lost a leg; Generals Bakhmetiev II and Aleksopol were badly wounded, General Ostermann was slightly wounded.

Defrance's division should have passed left of the redoubt together with (Wathier's) cuirassiers, but was late coming up. Meanwhile, Latour-Maubourg's Cavalry Corps came around the left side of the redoubt. Rozniecki's [4th Polish Light Cavalry] Ulan division, in two ranks, formed the right wing of the assault; the cuirassiers were the left wing; in the centre were the horse artillery batteries.

The Saxon Gardes du Corps went for the Redoubt, the Saxon Cuirassier Regiment Zastrow and the Polish Cuirassier Regiment Malachowski and the Westphalian cuirassier brigade charged the Infantry Regiments Pernau, Kexholm, and the 33rd Jaegers who were to the left in the valley. Our Russian infantry fired a volley at 60 paces; the enemy cavalry fled.

General Thielemann and the Saxon Gardes du Corps went over the ditch and the rampart into the redoubt. The general officer in command of the defence of the redoubt, General Likhachev, was in the redoubt. He was sick and also wounded, and was captured when the place was taken.

Likhachev's presentation to Napoleon following his capture is the subject of a dramatic oil painting, set in the usual 'Alpine' landscape and lit by the heavenly spotlights so beloved of those who were commissioned to immortalise the Emperor's conquests. It seems that Napoleon wished to return to Likhachev his sword, which had been taken from him, in recognition of his gallant defence of the Battery. Beckoning to an aide, who had accompanied Likhachev into his presence, Napoleon took the extra sword that the man was holding and proffered it to the captured general. Not recognising his own weapon, Likhachev refused to accept it. Apparently, linguistic difficulties prevented a clarification of the situation. Napoleon, becoming impatient at the embarrassing situation in which he found himself, muttered: 'Take this idiot away!'

Unbelievable as it may seem, in the midst of the blood bath and mayhem of the final struggle for the Battery, the Russian artillery managed to bring four of the 12-pounder pieces out and to bring them to the rear. Bogdanovich continues:

> At this point, Prince Eugène reached the redoubt with his infantry (the divisions of Morand, Gérard, and Broussier) and put the 9e *Ligne* [of the 14th Division] into it as garrison.
>
> Barclay de Tolly ordered the 24th Division to retake the redoubt from the valley to the east of it. Malachowski's cuirassiers charged the advancing Russians in their left flank. The charge was beaten off but Barclay now ordered a withdrawal behind the Gorizi [*sic*] stream.
>
> Enemy cavalry now prepared to charge the squares of the IV and VI Corps. A Polish Ulan regiment attacked the Russian foot artillery battery in which General Kostenetski, commander of the artillery of the VI Corps found himself. Kostenetski was a tall, strongly built man; he seized a rammer and led a counter-attack by the gunners to drive the Polish cavalry off.
>
> Most of Barclay's cavalry had been detached to our left wing earlier in the day, so he now had to conduct his defence with only infantry and artillery, but – at Barclay's orders – the Chevalier Guard and the Horse Guards under Major-General Shevich came up from the reserve and took post behind a small hill before Kniaskovo.
>
> Prince Eugène's IV Corps, Defrance's 4th Cuirassier Division, Chastel's 3rd Light Cavalry Division, and the 7e Dragons (of La Haussaye's 6th Cuirassier Division) now attacked Kaptsevich's 7th Division in front and rear [in its location north of the Battery]. Defrance's Carabiniers rode down a square of the 19th Jaeger Regiment.
>
> At this point, the 2nd Division [section] of the 2nd Guards Horse Artillery Battery, of Lieutenant Baron Korf, came up from the Reserve to the right-hand side of the Chevalier Guard. Seeing the defeat of the Jaegers, Korf – on his own initiative – advanced to within 300 metres [330 yd] of the enemy, unlimbered, opened up with canister, and drove the enemy back.
>
> Only Chastel's Light Cavalry Brigade remained on the field and these now charged at Korf's battery. Korf appealed at once to the commander of the 1st Troop, right-wing squadron of the Chevalier Guards [of the 1st Cuirassier Division]: 'Bashmakov! Save my guns!' The Chevalier Guard charged and drove off Chastel's brigade, saving the battery.
>
> Now Barclay came up and ordered the Chevalier Guard to undertake another charge. Colonel Löwenwold (the commander) formed his regiment by squadrons, advanced through the intervals of the squares of the 19th and 40th Jaegers and charged at the enemy cavalry of Thielemann's brigade. These were formed up with the Saxon Gardes du Corps and the Cuirassier Regiment Zastrow in the first rank, with two Polish lancer regiments in the second.

As the Russians closed with the enemy, they were received with a discharge of canister; Löwenwold fell, killed by a canister ball to the head. Colonel Levachov took over command at once but the momentum of the charge had been broken. [Apparently, this incident was only one of many such clashes between the Saxons and the Chevalier Guard that took place in this closing phase of the battle to the south-east of the Battery; von Schreckenstein tells us that, eventually, the Russians had the best of it and the Saxons retired.]

Renewed cavalry charges by the Chevalier Guard and the Horse Guards stabilised the situation [to the south-east of the Battery when the Izmail and Lithuanian Guards of the 11th Infantry Division – in six battalion squares – withdrew east across the valley to their new position on the ridge south of Gorki].

Enemy pressure on Barclay de Tolly increased; Barclay ordered General Adjutant Korf's II Cavalry Corps to advance [on his northern flank] to help him hold on. Korf sent Major-General Pantshulidsev II with the Iziumsk Hussars and the Polish Ulan Regiment who were sent against Wathier's cuirassiers and Defrance's Carabiniers. Their charge was beaten off but they rallied quickly.

Korf now sent Colonel Sass's Pskov Dragoons, with the Moscow Dragoons in support, to assault the right-hand side [north] of the Raevsky Battery. On the way there, Sass saw enemy infantry and cavalry threatening the right flank of the Iziumsk Hussars and the Polish Ulans. He at once charged the enemy cavalry (it may have been the 7e Dragons) and – having put them to flight – continued on towards his original target. He was now involved in a clash with enemy cavalry in which the French were eventually beaten back.

The Dragoon Regiment Pskov and the 1st Division, 2nd Guards Horse Artillery Battery, under Colonel Kosen, now assaulted the enemy's left-wing battalion, but a twelve-gun French battery caused them heavy loss and the attack failed.

The III Cavalry Corps now came up with the Sumy and Mariupol Hussars, the Orenburg, Siberian and Irkutsk Dragoons. Supported by part of the II Cavalry Corps, they charged the enemy cavalry masses. There followed a violent cavalry mêlée. Barclay de Tolly and his staff were right in the middle of it. One of Barclay's adjutants, Count Lamsdorf, was killed by an enemy pistol shot.

On the French side, Generals Chastel, Huard, and Gérard were killed; Grouchy and Domanget were wounded.

Prince Eugène's IV Corps now had control of the Raevsky Battery and the ridge on which it stood.

It was now 4 o'clock. The Russian army was in a line, 1200 paces east of the Raevsky Battery, east of the Gorizka valley. The right wing was at Gorki, the left wing was a cannon shot east of Semenovskaya, on the edge of the woods. The fighting now died away, except on the southern flank.

Thus ended this epic and costly struggle. Both sides had given more than their all. The cost in blood had been tremendous; the result – a draw.

Incredible as it may appear, there were troops on both sides who had not been engaged in this battle. On the allied side, it was the Imperial Guard which Napoleon refused repeatedly to commit to the battle despite the urgent entreaties of his marshals. This included Claparède's Legion of the Vistula, which had been brought forward in the afternoon but not actually thrown into the combat. Delzon's 13th Division was also reasonably intact. This gave a total of about 25,000 men.

The opinion of posterity has come down on Napoleon's side in this decision; as he said, he was not going to risk his last reserve so far from home unless it was absolutely necessary.

On the Russian side, the 4th, 30th, 34th, and 48th Jaegers (on the extreme right wing behind Gorki) had not been engaged all day. The Preobrazhensky and Semenovsky Guards Infantry Regiments had not been committed, and there were 15,000 Militia, Uvarov's I Cavalry Corps, and Platov's Cossacks which had scarcely been engaged. The Artillery Reserve of the 1st Army had also been largely unemployed, but had suffered considerable damage and casualties as it stood idly on the ridge behind Kniaskovo. In all, there were some 28,000 relatively fresh troops still available, due more to luck and mismanagement than skill.

16

The Aftermath – the Reckoning

AS DUSK FELL, the firing died away all along the opposing lines. Because the open throat of the Battery offered no protection to the allied troops who now held it from the Russian artillery fire from the ridge to the east, the infantry of Eugène's IV Corps abandoned it again. Whether this was a spontaneous action of self-preservation is not known, but it seems incredible that any responsible commander in the IV Corps would have knowingly ordered such a move. Certainly, Eugène had such a fear of incurring Napoleon's wrath that he would never have dared to countermand the Emperor's orders to capture (and to hold) the place.

Be that as it may, Barclay de Tolly – in his taking stock of the status of his 1st Army as evening fell – was told that the Battery was empty, and he gave orders that it should be reoccupied and that a new battery should be built that night.

Despite the pounding that his 1st Army had taken this day, Barclay's spirit and understanding of the situation were such that he was fully prepared to continue the fight next day. Schubert tells us that Barclay rode past him on his way to report to Kutuzov and called out to him that he should 'Report to me at 3 o'clock tomorrow morning and I will give you the orders for tomorrow's attack'.

Schubert continues:

> But as the reports came in from the various corps and divisions, it became clear that we were missing up to 50,000 men. Many generals and commanding officers had been wounded or killed. The artillery was in the worst state; many of the horses had been killed, much of the equipment and vehicles damaged, the first line ammunition stocks were almost exhausted and the replenishment parks were some days' march to the rear.
>
> And what of the losses? No-one knew the real figures then and no-one knows them now. All I can say, is that in the spring of 1813, we found about 50,000 human corpses on the battlefield.

Barclay gave orders for the reorganisation of his troops and sent his ADC, Colonel Volzogen to report to Kutuzov. By this time, both Barclay and

Volzogen knew the actual state of the 1st Army; when Volzogen appeared before Kutuzov, he blurted out the extremely unvarnished truth as he knew it. He only got as far as saying that all the vital points on his front were in enemy hands and that the regiments of the 1st Army had been battered to the point that they were no longer capable of offensive action, when he was interrupted by a furious Kutuzov; as Volzogen recalled in his memoirs, Kutuzov shouted at him:

> At which common sutleress's cart have you been getting drunk all day that you dare to give me such a report?
> As far as the state of the battle is concerned, I must be the best informed! All enemy attacks have been repelled all along the front. Tomorrow morning, I will set myself at the head of the army and at once drive the enemy from the soil of Holy Russia!

And, in fact, Kutuzov initially reported to the Tsar that the battle was a victory. He now dictated orders to Barclay to prepare for a renewed attack on 8 September.

After dark, he went to Tatarinovo, in the area now occupied by the remnants of Bagration's 2nd Army. Toll had preceded him and now reported that there was 'No hope' of this formation engaging in offensive action next day. The 2nd Army had lost about 20,000 casualties at Borodino. With fifty-four battalions, fifty-two squadrons, and twelve batteries, it now had only 14,000 men present and fit for duty including 8–9000 infantry. The six grenadier battalions which had defended the Bagration *flèches* now numbered only 300 men in all. The Cuirassier Regiment Astrakhan had started the day with 400 horses; it now had ninety-five. As Toll approached a group of infantry in the gloom, he asked, 'Which regiment is this?' The answer came back: 'We are the 2nd Grenadier Division'.

The Duke of Württemberg recorded that his 4th Division entered the combat with 3600 men that day; they suffered almost two-thirds killed and wounded. He also said that the 24th and 26th Divisions of the VI and VII Corps of the 2nd Army had been equally badly mauled. Concerning the severity of the Russian casualties, the Duke attributed them to:

> Poor tactical training (we had very many raw recruits), not making use of the terrain, and too dense a battle formation. The first and second lines of the infantry were only 200 paces apart, the cavalry were only 300 to 400 paces behind the infantry, and the reserves were only 1000 paces behind the cavalry.

It became clear that the Russian army could not afford to stay in the proximity of the enemy next day, let alone hope to continue the struggle at the Borodino site.

At 3 o'clock on the morning of 8 September, Kutuzov issued orders for a withdrawal. That night, the Russian army withdrew to a new position at Mozhaisk. The army's strength rose to about 50,000 men. A rearguard, consisting of the Cossacks, four Jaeger regiments of the II Corps, and the Infantry Regiments Tobolsk and Volhynia, stayed on the battlefield overnight. They rejoined the army at Mozhaisk at midday on 8 September.

According to Bogdanovich:

. . . the official casualty return of the 1st Army, they list the following casualties on 5 and 7 September:

	Generals	Officers	Enlisted Men	Total
Killed	3	213	9,036	9,252
Wounded	14	1,223	17,989	19,226
Missing	1	46	9,981	10,028
			less than 1000 were captured	
Total				38,506

No such report exists for the 2nd Army as most of the commanders had been killed or wounded, but if we accept the figure of 20,000 casualties as being roughly valid, then the total Russian losses for 5 and 7 September were approximately 58,000 men. Russian losses at Shevardino had been 6000; 8–10,000 stragglers rejoined their colours within the next few days, thus the loss at Borodino itself was about 40,000.

On the day that the Russian army evacuated Moscow, they mustered 80,000 men including 53,000 line troops and they had received no fresh reinforcements since Borodino.

The generals killed were; Bagration (died on 24 September), Tuchkov I, Kutaisov, and Tuchkov IV. The wounded were: Ermolov, Ostermann, Prince Karl von Mecklenburg, St Priest, Prince Gorchakov, Bakhmetiev I, Bakhmetiev II, Neverovsky, Vorontsov, Likhachev, Stavitsky, Kern, De Rossi, Schreider, Matsniev, Ivelich, Zibulsky, and Aleksopol.

If the Russians were in a battered state, the allies were practically no better off as will be seen. The Westphalian officer, Conrady, left us his impression of that night on the battlefield.

The shadows of night and a damp, cold mist crept over the bloody field, hiding it from the eyes of the survivors. Out there lay many thousands of brave soldiers sleeping the eternal sleep, but many more lay with shattered limbs, wracked with pain and thirst, waiting for aid but in vain. It was not feasible to think about mounting a rescue operation, except that each unit could care for those wounded who lay in their immediate vicinity. Happy were those who had received a quick bullet or sabre cut!

We had won, but we had no joy in our victory.

Once again, there was absolutely no organisation to care for the wounded and these died in their thousands of thirst or of lack of care. This utterly hopeless situation eventually led to officers commanding units to carry out mercy killings on the obviously hopeless cases.

It is extremely difficult to be accurate about the losses of either side in this massive battle; even those fragmentary parade states which were produced on 8 September were probably only about 60 per cent valid, so great was the confusion and the dissolution of the regiments that had taken part in the fighting. Of these records, the great majority was to be lost or destroyed (accidentally or deliberately as fire-lighters) during the retreat. All loss calculations for Borodino are, at best, 'guess-timates'.

On the allied side [according to Déniée], their total losses amounted to 28,000 all ranks killed, wounded, and missing at Borodino on 7 September itself. These included twelve generals, ten colonels, 6547 officers and men killed, thirty-seven generals, twenty-seven colonels, 21,453 officers and men wounded.

We may obtain some idea of the casualties suffered by the *Grande Armée* on the basis of the examples reproduced below.

Roth von Schreckenstein gives us the following states of General von Thielemann's brigade:

	6 September	8 September
Saxon Gardes du Corps	450 horses	103 horses
Saxon Zastrow Cuirassiers	400 horses	136 horses
Polish 14th Cuirassier Regiment	180 horses	95 horses
A further 86 horses were collected this day		86 horses
Totals	*1030 horses*	*420 horses*

The total loss of enlisted men in the battle was 287 killed and missing, 323 wounded, mostly seriously. Among the officers, the figures were: thirty-nine dead and twenty-nine wounded (including two captured). There were thus 652 casualties.

Hiller's horse artillery battery lost twelve men and twenty-three horses and fired 600 shots during the action. Some of the ignition holes in the cannon were by now so burned out, that Hiller had serious doubts as to whether the guns could be used safely.

Von Ditfurth tells us that the Württemberg Leib-Chevaux-légèrs Regiment went into the battle with 386 horses on the morning of 7 September; next day, they could muster only sixty-three and had thus lost 84 per cent. The Württemberg infantry started with 1456 all ranks and lost fifteen officers and 259 men, or 19 per cent.

The Bavarians fared no better. General Count von Preysing-Moos (commanding the 3rd, 4th, 5th, and 6th Chevaux-légèrs Regiments) recorded in his diary that his division lost five officers and over 100 men and 100 horses during 7 September. The 1st and 2nd Chevaux-légèrs, in Domanget's 17th Light Cavalry Brigade, III Cavalry Corps, came out of the battle with only six officers and twenty-nine men fit for duty between them!

According to Preysing, 'The repeated, murderous assaults on the Bagration *flèches* were responsible for the destruction of the greatest part of the French [allied] cavalry.'

In the VIII Westphalian Corps they had lost 3000 killed, wounded, and missing; most of the wounded subsequently died of starvation, neglect, or disease. Two-thirds of the officers had been wounded and eighteen killed. Some regiments suffered enormous losses: Lieutenant Wagner's regiment went into action 1600 strong; on 8 September, they mustered scarcely 700.

The Jaeger-Carabiniers of the Westphalian Guard started the day with 550 men; that evening they were down to between thirty and forty. Conrady's regiment lost nine officers and 397 men; von Linsingen's battalion mustered 700 all ranks in the morning; by that night they had lost ten officers and 341 men.

The entire VIII Corps lost 500 killed (including eighteen officers) and 2500 wounded (including 164 officers) according to von Borcke. The official losses, published in the Westphalian *Moniteur* on 10 October, were 300 dead and 1000 wounded.

The Poles of V Corps lost over 1000 killed, wounded, and missing during the day.

Some of the generals killed were: Montbrun, Caulaincourt, Compère, Huard, Lanabere, Morion, Plauzonne, Romeuf, von Breunning, Damas, von Lepel and Chastel. Those wounded included: Marshal Davout Rapp, Nansouty, Grouchy, Morand, Friant, Desaix, Compans, Beliard, Tharreau, St Germain, Bruyère, Pajol, Defrance, Scheeler, Bonamy. Lahoussaye, Alméras, Sokolnicki, Bordessoulle, Bessières, von Borstell, le Rebeval, Chlopicki, Chouard, Domanguet, Dufour, Gengoult, Legras, Hammerstein, von Wickenberg, Krasinski, Queunot, Mourier, Suberwiecz, Teste, Thury, Triaire, D'Henin, Cattaneo, Burthe.

Larrey gives total losses at Shevardino and Borodino as 22,000; Thiers states 30,000. However, after Borodino, the *Grande Armée* mustered only

100,000 officers and men; their loss must therefore have been not less than that of the Russians.

The number of guns taken was roughly equal at about seventeen each; no colours or standards were taken.

Prince Eugen of Württemberg had the following reflective words to say about the battle:

> A dear friend of mine, whose ashes have long since been consigned to the earth, wrote the following about Borodino: 'To be honest, Kutuzov had no cause to have Alexander hold a Te Deum [a holy mass of thanksgiving], neither did Napoleon have cause to write a victorious report to his Empress. If we warriors could have forgotten the quarrels of the great men and shaken hands over the altar of justice next day, Fama (the Roman goddess of Fame) would have recognised us as twins.'

After a brief rest to reorganise what was left of the *Grande Armée*, the chase was on again to catch and destroy the remnants of the 'beaten' Russian army. The VIII (Westphalian) Corps was left with the unenviable job of clearing up the battlefield; their efforts were as nothing considering the scale of the task.

17

The Russian Campaign after Borodino

ON 10 SEPTEMBER NAPOLEON'S advance guard under Murat clashed with the Russian rearguard under General Miloradovich (Baggovut's II Corps) at Mozhaisk, about 10 miles (16 km) east of Borodino. Mozhaisk today is a completely soulless collection of concrete blocks of flats and industrial premises; only the ornate Byzantine church gives any indication of the long history of the town. In 1812 it was, presumably, the usual grouping of primitive log cabins and barns. Losses in this affair were about equal at 2000 killed, wounded, and missing on each side: no guns or trophies changed hands.

Kutuzov continued on eastwards towards Moscow, abandoning some 10,000 wounded from the battles of 5 and 7 September because of the lack of transport with which to move them. A planning conference of the Russian Imperial General Staff was held to consider the feasibility of standing again, west of Moscow; but the severe losses of Borodino, and the need for time to be given to the shattered regiments to regroup and to absorb reinforcements, dictated that another major battle should be avoided for some weeks. Reluctantly, Kutuzov recommended to the Tsar that Moscow be evacuated and left to Napoleon.

Hitherto, this had always been the breaking point for Napoleon's opponents. Potential loss of their capital city, Vienna, had forced the Austrians to knuckle under in 1805 and 1809; this time, Alexander was determined that the story should be different. The main problem for the Austrians in earlier years had been that they were in danger of running out of strategic space in which to manoeuvre once their capital, with its major arsenals, fortifications (even if obsolete), and population concentration, fell into enemy hands. The Austrian court also lacked the traditional Slavic ruthlessness of the Tsars, and the Austrian people lacked the traditional Slavic fatalism of the citizens of Alexander's capital city. Confident that the order would be obeyed, such fatalism allowed the Russian government to order Moscow's inhabitants to leave behind everything that they could not carry and to trek off into the vast, thinly populated forests to the south, east, and north of the city.

Napoleon would take Moscow, that the Tsar could not prevent. But Alexander could – and did – minimise the advantages that the most powerful man in the world could wring from his prize.

When Napoleon reached the outskirts of Moscow on 14 September, he was disconcerted at the unusual silence that greeted his arrival, and by the absence of the usual, subservient, nervous deputation of city dignitaries, eagerly proffering him the keys of the prostrate and helpless town. Patrols, which he had sent out in several directions, soon confirmed the incredible and unpalatable truth: the city was all but empty; only the non-Russian foreigners and some of the lowest classes had remained behind. For the first time, Napoleon was confronted with the fact that *he* was no longer the centre of the universe, was no longer the arbiter of events on the world's stage. The strings with which he usually manipulated the puppet-like pygmies who dwelt in his world had suddenly and deftly been cut, and he had not even heard the snip of the scissors. By sacrificing his capital city, Alexander had wrested the strategic and moral initiative from the invader. Not in his wildest dreams had Napoleon imagined that the Russians could possibly abandon Moscow. ('A good general may be defeated, but he should never be surprised!')

Perhaps without knowing it, the young Tsar had become the first – and possibly the only – one of the omnipotent Napoleon's enemies to have outwitted him so utterly. To say that Napoleon was left this day, at the gates of Moscow, figuratively open jawed and with egg on his face, would be no overstatement.

In deflated mood, his cavalcade walked through the empty, echoing streets, through this strange city, the meeting place of Europe and Asia, with its China Town, oriental trading quarter east of the Kremlin. That great, ancient, brick-built, red fortress stood on the slight hill to the north of the River Moskva (almost enclosed in a loop of the river) with its distinctly non-European battlements and its plethora of gilded, Byzantine church towers rising high into the sky.

Surprisingly enough, even today many of Moscow's buildings are still built of logs covered with a plaster or cement rendering; their secrets are revealed only if they catch fire or are demolished as the city modernises. In 1812, only the Kremlin and the area immediately to the north and east were brick built and enclosed by high, medieval walls. The rest of the sprawling city was almost entirely built of wood. Several fires in the past had laid waste to whole districts at a time. The city maintained a well-developed and equipped fire-fighting organisation. In the evacuation which had just been carried out, however, the Governor of Moscow, Count Rostopchin, had ensured that all such fire-fighting equipment was also removed. Thus, the city would be utterly defenceless if a fire should break out.

Even before Napoleon's entry into the city, fire had broken out in several different quarters and was rapidly raging out of control, to such an extent that, until the fires had burnt themselves out, Napoleon and his entourage had to evacuate the Kremlin and move up the road towards St Petersburg to take up temporary residence in one of the Tsar's hunting lodges a few miles out.

At once, the French blamed Russian arsonists for the destruction, and scores of hapless Muscovites were rounded up, tried by courts martial, and shot. Whatever their guilt or innocence (and, to this day, the truth has not been established), the French army had survived for years by *marauder* (looting and pillaging), and it has repeatedly been recorded by contemporary eye-witnesses that it was the usual custom of such *marauders* to set fire to any premises that they had finished looting. Carelessness with cooking fires, and the ready availability of wine and spirits in the abandoned houses were also factors contributing to the destruction of so much material that could have been of service to the *Grande Armée* in the coming winter.

The Bavarian general, the Count Maximilian von Preysing-Moos (commanding the 21st Light Cavalry Brigade) records these dramatic events as follows:

> On 13 September we continued our advance, crossed the Moskva at the village of Paskoya, and took post in front of a large wood. Late in the evening Grouchy's III Cavalry Corps arrived; it was 1400 to 1600 horses strong. My two Chevaux-légers regiments now numbered only twenty-nine files together [this means that the two regiments now had only fifty-eight troopers and NCOs between them; in early July they had numbered 986!]. When we moved off next morning at 7 o'clock, we were followed by General La Haussaye's (6th Dragoon) Division. In the closely wooded country the Cossacks attacked us with much more severity than in the past few days. At one point they mounted a determined charge at our advanced guard, giving out a great cheer as they did so. Initially, our troops were overwhelmed and gave ground, before rallying and driving the enemy back. My 4th Regiment suffered some wounded, the Chasseurs had considerable losses.
>
> The enemy appeared to be determined to oppose our crossing of the Moskva [the river meanders considerably in this area, and the road would have crossed it several times] but fell back after exchanging a few shells with us when our outflanking move developed. We took post at the village of Khorokhova. From our picket line, despite the unclear weather, we had a good view of the mighty city of Moscow and, even on this day, we could see several great fires burning, which we took to be the destruction of military magazines.
>
> Before we marched off at 7 o'clock on the morning of 15 September,

an Order of the Day was given out whereby no one was to enter the city until further notice. [This was the day after Napoleon's arrival at the deserted gates.] With Guyon's Light Cavalry Brigade in the lead, we marched to the left around Moscow, making a halt of some hours at the village of Dvorets to gather news of the progress of the other columns. During the recent marches, even in this well-urbanised area and so close to such a great city, there had been no sight of living human beings, and the destruction of all food and forage supplies – and even the buildings – was much greater than heretofore. The newly ripened grain had been deliberately trodden down, all the stacks of straw and hay were in flames, and huge clouds of smoke poured up out of Moscow itself.

Our march continued directly past one of the city gates without our seeing a living soul, and we took up a miserable bivouac in a village called Maria Rostoka. One squadron took post on the road to Moscow. General Ornano sent out two pickets each of thirty men; one of these soon came haring back, hotly pursued right into our lines, by sixty or seventy Cossacks. The 5th Regiment had seven men wounded in this mêlée, and lost five men and eight horses captured. I reinforced this picket with thirty men, deployed them in a more defensible manner and, from then on, the situation remained quiet. The Viceroy [Eugène] took up residence in the fine St Petersburg suburb.

On 16 September we sent out patrols at 4 in the morning but they found no trace of the enemy. One officer from each regiment received permission to go into Moscow; flour was distributed to the men.

On 17, at 6 in the morning, we rode through the village of Aleksyevskaya, crossed the Yausa stream [they were now on the eastern side of the city] where a company of infantry was detached, and went on to the village of Rastokino where we halted to await further orders. At 4 in the afternoon these arrived; we set the village of Aleksyevskaya into a state of defence, and each regiment sent a party of one officer and sixteen men into Moscow to be issued with food. [This is what Preysing wrote. I strongly doubt that a formal system of collection and distribution of rations was ever set up by the French in Moscow; it was the usual case of 'every man for himself'!] Later that night, the fires in Moscow raged to such an extent that even Napoleon himself had to leave the Kremlin at 1 in the morning.

In the following days we sent out reconnaissance missions as well as the normal local patrols; General Ornano moved his headquarters further to the rear, into the magnificent palace of Astankina, property of the Count Sheremetev [to the north of the city and spelled 'Ostankino'], but I stayed with my brigade as the extreme outpost line in Aleksyevskaya. On 21 September a Spanish battalion moved into the village to reinforce our garrison.

On 22 the entire army was supposed to move off, but the order was cancelled. During the next three days everything was quiet but we saw several villages in the neighbourhood going up in flames. Moscow itself had been completely burned down. [This is not so: about a quarter to a third of the city's buildings survived the conflagration.]

On 26 I marched with my division through Moscow, along the road towards Mozhaisk to Pershushkino, six hours from that town, to secure communications with the King of Naples and to the rear. General Broussier's (14th Infantry) Division – which I was supporting – stayed one hour behind me in the village of Yasky; between us, at Yudina, was a regiment of Chasseurs of the Imperial Guard under General Guyot.

On 28 the entire light cavalry of the IV Corps mounted a reconnaissance to the village of Fedosino without making contact with the enemy. We bivouacked in misery in a small wood near Broussier's Division. This night and the next were so cold, the weather so wet and windy, and no food or forage available, that we were forced to seek better shelter in the devastated village of Yudina. There we were at least able to find a church that could be heated in which to put the wounded and sick. On 30 we sent back to Moscow Major Gaddum, an ensign, and ten men who were seriously ill; seven officers, forty-six men, fifty-nine sick horses, eighty-eight un-mounted men, and fifty-seven gunners were sent to the hospital in Rusa.

From 1 to 15 October, nothing of note occurred; we sent out patrols on a daily basis and also larger detachments, with artillery support, to escort couriers or to scavenge supplies and forage from the surrounding countryside. In this period, the weather was fine and as mild as it would have been in our homeland. . . . The Russians exploited this apparent operational pause to reinforce and redeploy their forces, to occupy the best positions on our flanks and in our rear, to cut all our communications, and to make our scavenging missions as difficult and costly as possible. At the same time, they maintained a façade of negotiations [with the Emperor] purposefully dragged out for as long as possible, to hold us in our extended position until winter should strike us and cause that terrible catastrophe which, let it be stated, was now inevitable anyway.

Our army dwindled away daily through the combined effects of hunger, sickness, deprivation, and exhaustion. Our reinforcements could not fight their way through from the west to reach us and, since 14 October, the frosts had set in with a vengeance.

Finally, on 15 October, we began our withdrawal. My 3rd and 6th Regiments were detached to General Ornano. With the rest, and the battery, I joined Broussier's Division and we set off on the road to Kaluga to bivouac in the village of Sharapova. After a march of four hours, we heard cannon and small arms fire from ahead. We sent out a patrol which reported that Ornano's baggage train had been ambushed by several hundred Cossacks as a result of the lax conduct of the escort. Many people had been cut down and killed or wounded, and part of the convoy plundered. We hurried to reach the scene but could capture only a single Cossack. We marched on to Fominskya where the infantry halted. I took my cavalry and a battalion of Spaniards, and took post half-an-hour ahead at the village of Malkovo.

On 17 October Ornano took the light cavalry, a regiment of infantry, and two guns on a reconnaissance in strength towards the west. After an hour's march, we were attacked by several Cossack groups; after some skirmishing (which cost me some wounded) we returned to camp in the afternoon.

On the information of a peasant whom we had captured – that 10 versts [6.6 miles (10.7 km)] to our left-hand side was an enemy force of four infantry and two cavalry regiments – I received on 18 October the task of taking two cavalry regiments, 300 infantry, and one gun to reconnoitre in their direction. Just before we moved off, however, the Chasseur outposts were attacked and driven back into the village. General alarm was sounded and we all rushed to our predetermined posts. Mine was on the left flank with the 5th and 6th Regiments. Several regiments of enemy cavalry were advancing against us, and I was forced to form a hook by refusing my flank. This move was scarcely completed when we were attacked on three sides by a force of dragoons, lancers, and Cossacks, to the number of about 1500 men, who charged at us whooping wildly. As my two regiments together numbered only about 400 men, and as it was impossible to goad our exhausted horses into a trot, I was forced to receive this charge standing. With admirable cool-headedness, my men took aim with their carbines and let the enemy charge up to within 15 paces of them. This steady conduct, and the shell and canister fire of two of our guns, which had come up in our support, caused the enemy to break off the charge and retire into a nearby wood, taking some wounded with him and leaving some dead men and horses on the field. In the meantime, the 9e *Chasseurs à Cheval* had been overthrown and driven back with heavy loss. As this exposed my rear, I was forced to order the second rank of the 6th Regiment to turn about; this made my situation, in such close proximity to the enemy, even more perilous. Thus we remained until dark. The spare horses and the baggage were sent back to Fominskya where the wagons were formed into a circle.

At 4 o'clock on the morning of 19 October, the picket of the Chasseurs was again attacked by Russian hussars and forced back on to the infantry who were able to drive the enemy off with the loss of one officer and several hussars wounded.

That afternoon, a meeting took place between the outposts of General Ornano and General Miloradovich during which the latter claimed to have defeated the King of Naples the previous day with heavy loss. At dusk we began our withdrawal in utter silence, but had only crossed the Nava stream when the order was countermanded. We had to drive off the Cossacks who had been following us and force our way back into the village of Malkovo which we had just left. The weather was appalling, we were worn out with fatigue. It was only the hope of soon getting to a better climate in the Ukraine or Volhynia that kept us going.

On the evening of 20 October, news reached us that the King of Naples had, in fact, been ambushed on 18 October at Tarutino and forced into a three-hour withdrawal with the loss of many guns.

This first-hand account of some of the events that took place during Napoleon's stay in Moscow gives us an accurate portrait – in miniature – of what happened to the entire *Grande Armée* in this critical period. Napoleon knew the sorry state of his army quite well enough to have no further illusions about his possible courses of action now. The great horde with which he had invaded Russia had melted away, day by day, during the long trek to Moscow, a destination that was not even on his itinerary for 1812 when he had crossed the border less than twelve weeks ago. The condition of Grouchy's corps was a typical case in point. On 5 July the parade-states had shown 6076 horses present and fit for duty; on 13 September, it had dwindled to 'between 1400 and 1600 horses' or 25 per cent of its former strength. In modern military operational planning, any unit or formation that loses more than 50 per cent of its strength is considered to be no longer capable of effective tactical use. Apart from the Imperial Guard, which had – as usual – been pampered and preserved from contact with the enemy or from the privations to which the rest of the army had been exposed, all other corps in and around Moscow were nothing more than ghosts of their former selves.

Napoleon had dithered his way into Moscow and was now stuck there, hoping that the Tsar would be stupid enough to throw him a lifeline as he had at Austerlitz in 1805. For, if the Tsar did not, Napoleon was completely at his mercy. Not only were his troops still dwindling away before his eyes, but the balance of power was tilting, with increasing speed, in the favour of the Russians. As Preysing-Moos so correctly put it, the Russians exploited the lull in operations to the full. The four weeks that Napoleon spent in Moscow must have been the most frustrating and humiliating of his life until then – St Helena was yet to come!

There was no question of his marching out of Moscow to challenge the Russians in the open field to a second Borodino. His sword was broken; he would have to try his penmanship. He sent repeated peace offers and letters to the Tsar. They remained unanswered or were replied to with vague inconsequentialities in evasive tone, tantalisingly dangling the hopes of serious negotiations before Napoleon's nose while the Russian army bound up its wounds, called up, trained, and equipped new recruits, repaired or replaced its artillery, replenished its ammunition supplies, and mobilised guerrilla forces on the flanks and rear of the invaders.

Extensive militia forces were raised in all the western provinces of Russia. There was a genuine upsurge of patriotic fervour among all classes of their society, whipped up to fever pitch by the priests of the Orthodox Church, who convinced their willing flocks that Napoleon was the Antichrist and that his men were all infidels. A common militia badge at this time was the cross in various forms, one version of which was adopted in Prussia for their Landwehr regiments in 1813–15.

It is a little-known fact that recognition of the heroic national struggle of the Spanish people against their French oppressors in the years from 1808 to 1813 served as a model for similar partisan groupings in Russia in 1812. Built around a small core of – initially – a squadron or two of Cossacks or hussars 'cadged' from Kutuzov, these small, highly mobile groups, led by the likes of Davidov, 'swam in the waters of the population' in the areas abutting the outer fringes of the *Grande Armée*, nipping and snapping at the French heels, capturing couriers and despatches, picking off sentries, killing small foraging parties, overrunning small outposts, disrupting the enemy's sleep with nightly alarms, destroying stocks of food and forage, and gathering operational intelligence from the local peasants who were only too willing to provide it for them, together with food and shelter. Martinien's invaluable listings of officer casualties of the French army show for this period in 1812 a series of entries – even for the cavalry regiments of the Imperial Guard – where one or two officers would be reported as killed or wounded on each occasion, thus testifying to the character of the daily life of the invaders at this time.

Morgenstern tells us that one battalion of the 6th Westphalian Infantry Regiment had been left as garrison in the town of Vereya. Despite repeated requests to Junot for reinforcements and artillery (all of which were denied despite being supported by General von Ochs), and a noticeable increase in the frequency and severity of enemy action around them, they were left in isolation. During the night of 10/11 October, they were attacked by a force of regular Russian troops, Cossacks, and militia, and overwhelmed. Only a handful escaped to tell the tale.

During Napoleon's fateful stay in Moscow, the city was surrounded with a screen of light forces designed to ensure that the invaders were kept on tenterhooks and ignorant of Russian plans and dispositions. The main Russian field army was concentrated to the south of the capital, around Tarutino and south of Podolsk, in a skilfully chosen flanking position to the *Grande Armée*'s axis of advance. As soon as Kutuzov judged that his army was again capable of serious operations against the French, he struck – at Tarutino (also known as Vinkovo) on 18 October. Miloradovich, with 36,000 men fell upon Murat (who had only 18,000 to hand) and inflicted casualties of 2000 killed and wounded and 1500 captured – as well as thirty-six guns – for his own losses of 800 killed and wounded and 700 – including General Baggovut – captured. ('A good general may be defeated but . . . '). Russian morale soared; that of the remaining invaders slumped.

This large-scale ambush finally caused the penny to drop in Napoleon's mind. There would be no peace in 1812. No one would be throwing him a life-line this time. He had carefully manoeuvred himself out on to this limb and into this critical situation, and must now fight his way out as best he could. The Emperor had embarked on the greatest game of bluff and counter-bluff in his career to date, and his younger opponent (Alexander was thirty-four to Napoleon's forty-three at this point) had outwitted him by enticing him into Moscow. Napoleon had made two major errors in this game: he had greatly underestimated his opponent; and he had begun to believe in his own propaganda of his invincibility. The stakes in this game had been incredibly high; with his bluff called, Napoleon – or more correctly, about 300,000 of his hapless followers – had paid, or were about to pay, for *his* mistakes . . . and with their lives. But, as Napoleon later remarked, 'What are the lives of half-a-million men to a man such as me?' The same question might have been asked with equally disarming sincerity by Adolf Hitler, Joseph Stalin, and Pol Pot. Indeed, a recent, major American biography of the Emperor states that several modern psychologists consider him to have been a psychopath.

So the sojourn in Moscow was over. The remnants of the *Grande Armée* hurriedly packed up their largely useless booty – most of which would be thrown away within days in an attempt to lighten the loads – and streamed out of the city in a vast convoy of gigs, coaches, carriages, and farm carts in a vain effort to reach the safety of western Europe. Napoleon left on 18 October; Marshal Mortier stayed on to mine the Kremlin but the resultant explosions were largely ineffective.

Even French historians are critical of Napoleon's squandering of his time in Moscow. The Count de Segur wrote:

How had it happened that in Moscow everything had been forgotten? Why was there so much useless baggage [on the retreat from the city]; why did so many soldiers die so soon of hunger and cold under the weight of their knapsacks which were full of gold instead of with food and clothing? Above all, why, in the thirty-three days, had not efforts been made to make snow shoes for the men and the horses? If these things had been done, we would not have lost our best men at the Vop, the Dnieper, and along the whole road. But why, in the absence of orders from Napoleon, had not these precautions been taken by his commanders, all of them kings, princes, and marshals? Had not the winter in Russia been foreseen? . . . The army left Moscow 100,000 strong; in twenty-five days it had been reduced to 36,000 men.

Segur put his finger on a very valid point here. Napoleon never groomed a successor. Neither did he encourage independent initiative or action by his underlings as is witnessed by his 'remote-control' mismanagement of the war in Spain from 1808 to 1813. In that conflict, he had placed his brother, Joseph (nominally King of Spain at Napoleon's behest) in an impossible situation by dividing Spain into several fiefdoms, each headed by one of his generals or marshals who reported directly to him, ignoring any 'orders' that Joseph might issue from Madrid. To Joseph remained only the unenviable role of the Emperor's whipping boy when things did not develop in accordance with the outdated schemes that Napoleon cooked up in France, northern Germany, or wherever he happened to be at the time the much-outdated despatches reached him from the rapidly changing battlefields of Spain.

His usually omnipotent genius and the ability to think of everything required for an operation without any input on the part of his staff and

Napoleon Bonaparte, Emperor of the French, leaving Moscow on 19 October 1812

Napoleon's conduct of his invasion of Russia was marked with bouts of indecision.

He wasted time in Vilnius early in the advance, and again at Smolensk. His stay in Moscow sealed the fate of the remnants of his army as he waited in vain to hear a reply from Alexander to his offer of peace.

A plate by Faber du Four who witnessed the scene. Author's collection

entourage seem to have deserted him in 1812. His 'kings, princes, and marshals' – long since used to being merely part of the backcloth of the stage on which he demonstrated his overpowering virtuosity – apparently did not notice his decline, or preferred to ignore it.

Initially, Napoleon headed south-west in the hope of avoiding the devastated corridor that was the trail of his advance from Vilnius, and of taking advantage of the warmer climes and unravaged farmlands of the Ukraine. In so doing, he callously abandoned to the tender mercies of the Russian partisans, all the increasingly isolated garrisons stretched along his old lines of communication. [In none of the accounts of the 1812 campaign, which I have read, have I found any mention of orders being sent to these unfortunates to concentrate anywhere to survive the winter, for them to fight their way out to the west, or to join up with the Emperor on his new, southerly line of operations. They were expendable; they had apparently outlived their usefulness.]

This 'dash for the sun' received an early setback, however, when, on 24 October, Kutuzov blocked Napoleon's path at Maloyaroslavets, 64 miles (103 km) south-west of Moscow. About 24,000 men were involved on each side; the action was extremely hard fought, mostly by the Italians of Eugène's IV Corps on the allied side. The allies lost 6000, the Russians 8000, but Napoleon's drive south was stopped. He turned back to the north-west and into the killing grounds that the Tsar had chosen for him.

But what of events in the other sectors of the combat zone? In Latvia, Marshal Macdonald bickered ineffectively outside Riga with General Essen's Russians, largely independent of events at Moscow; in the south a similarly low-key contest spluttered on through the summer, but Schwarzenberg was unable to hold his forward posture in mid-October and began to withdraw westwards under increasing Russian pressure. It was at Polotsk, on the northern flank of Napoleon's main thrust, that the most negative turn of events took place. Here, Marshals Oudinot and Saint Cyr, with the II and VI Corps, had, since July, been holding Wittgenstein's Russians away from the over-extended and vulnerable lines of communication stretching from Warsaw to Moscow. They had managed to hold off the Russians at the First Battle of Polotsk on 16–18 August but, while Wittgenstein's I Corps gathered its strength over the next weeks, the French, Swiss, and Bavarians opposing them lost more and more men through disease and starvation. Although they again held their ground at the Second Battle of Polotsk on 18–20 October, they were now so weak numerically – and the officers and men so demoralised – that they were forced to withdraw, fighting stubbornly, to the south-west.

So, the dwindling force that Napoleon led, joined up with their original entry route at the battlefield of Borodino on 30 October. Morgenstern, with the Westphalians of the VIII Corps, has left us a vivid picture of the nature of the retreat even in these early stages. We will follow him along parts of his desperate trek westwards; his account may be taken as being typical for thousands who were now fighting for their survival.

We bivouacked near the monastery of Kolozky. Despite the fact that the evacuation of the hospital here had been ordered well in advance, little had actually happened owing to the lack of transport. We saw the pitiful fear of those helpless sick and wounded as they watched the convoy passing them by, to leave them to the mercies of the vengeful Russians. We felt the bitterness of those seriously ill who now gave up all hope of being moved from their pestilential cells. The possibility that poor Maibom [a companion of Morgenstern's wounded at Borodino] might still be alive, drove me to enter the place. Chaotic disorder met me at every turn; there were no staff left to answer my questions! I had exposed myself to all those horrors for nothing.

The Emperor ordered that every vehicle in the endless convoy that streamed past the place should take as many sick and wounded with them as they could. The order extended to the sutlers' carts, to all the vehicles laden with the spoils of the city, and even to the coaches of the generals themselves. Any contravention was to be reported to the Provost Marshal who was authorised to confiscate all vehicles of the offending persons. In spite of this, the order had but little effect. The unwelcome guests were grudgingly taken on board but, within a few days, many such wagons vanished from the convoy; despite the perils from the ever-present Cossacks, the owners took the risk of slipping off for a day to dump their helpless loads in the forest at the first opportunity.

Morgenstern continues:

The bonds of discipline fell apart within the first few days of the retreat; a dreadful omen of what was to come. We marched through Gshazk, where we picked up our 3rd Battalion and on to Viasma. In Griednovo our 8th Infantry Regiment met us and on 3 November we reached Dorogobush, where we were granted a rest day.

The increasing cold and the hunger had decimated us to such an extent already that my company now numbered little over thirty men. The supplies which we had brought from Mozhaisk had long since been eaten and, apart from a little flour that we received in Viasma, no rations had been issued. We were thus forced to send out foraging parties, but they rarely found anything in this devastated strip of land and usually lost men in skirmishes with the Cossacks and the militia, or to desertion as the weaker individuals fell by the wayside or slipped off to try to make their way back alone.

In our bivouac at Dorogobush no one had anything to eat. The men's spirits were so low that I readily agreed to my sergeant's suggestion that we eat my horse. One of my NCOs had been a butcher in civilian life; he slaughtered and jointed the animal and divided it into rations for several days. Then we cooked, boiled, and fried it. I was presented with the choicest part, the tongue. This was the last ray of sunshine before we were engulfed by the impending catastrophe!

The rapidly increasing cold and the first snowfall that we had in the bivouac in Dorogobush pointed to the onset of an early winter. The main body of the army was close behind us and we often heard the sounds of distant cannon fire.

On 5 November we left Dorogobush. That same evening, we had a heavy snowfall; the snow fell in such large and dense flakes that even the nearest objects were unrecognisable. The wind raged and whipped the snow into deep drifts, covering ditches and streams into which the exhausted, heavily laden soldiers collapsed. Anyone who managed to climb out of one of these death-traps could count himself lucky. The icy blizzard whipped into our faces, blinding us. The snow balled up under our feet and found its way through every layer of clothing to melt on the skin so that we were soaked through and frozen. The muskets slipped from our frozen hands; winter was disarming and destroying us much more effectively and quickly than the enemy ever could!

The frost of 6 November and the following days thwarted all of Napoleon's plans. [This is patently not so! His plans – and his army – had been effectively reduced to ruins by the Battle of Borodino at the latest.]

All we could think of was to make it through to the magazines at Smolensk where we hoped to find food, shelter, clothing, and rest. . . . The greater part of our artillery had already had to be abandoned as the weakened draught horses dropped dead from fatigue. We spiked the guns, burned the carriages on the camp fires, and blew up the ammunition wagons. When we reached Smolensk, we were issued with rations for several days but ordered to march out at once to occupy a position on the flank of our retreating army to guard it against attack from the Russians. [The Westphalians were extremely lucky to have received rations in Smolensk; many of the starving wretches who followed them were turned away from the magazines with nothing by the French commissary officials because they could no longer prove that they belonged to any particular regiment.]

Morgenstern's generous act of sacrificing his horse for the common good paid handsome dividends:

When we left Mozhaisk, my company had been the weakest in the regiment; at Smolensk, with twenty-one men, it was the strongest. The cause of this seemed to me to be the fact that, as long as the men were convinced that they would receive food and protection with their unit, they would stay with their regiment; once there was no longer this prospect, they would desert and try to make their own way home, and nothing would keep them with their colours.

After two days on outpost duty, Morgenstern's company was ordered to a spot west of the town. That night, as the entire 2nd Battalion of his regiment was sleeping around a fire in the centre of a barn, all hell broke out when the fire got out of control and set off the cartridges in the men's packs. Fortunately, there were no casualties but many of the men lost their possessions and muskets; fortunately for them, too, the latter were quickly replaced with the weapons of the dead and sick.

Next day Morgenstern, his sergeant, and three men tried to go back into Smolensk to draw more rations from the magazines there. By now, the main body of the army was beginning to reach the town; at the prospect of food, the starving hordes lost all control and discipline, and stormed the place. Morgenstern described the scene as follows

The only thing to do in this chaos was to help ourselves. The conditions were far worse than any of the rumours that we had heard. We five, still fairly strong, men, clung together in the maelstrom of men, horses, and vehicles that were trying to squeeze through the narrow gateway into the city. We let ourselves be carried forward in the crush over the remains of wrecked vehicles, harness, discarded equipment, dead horses, and even human corpses. At the gate itself, however, any further progress was impossible. Formed bodies of armed troops cut their way into or out of the city with bayonet and butt; mounted men spurred their horses directly into the throng, regardless of whom or how many they trampled underfoot. By use of all our strength, we managed to extricate ourselves from this dangerous press to one side at the cost of some bruising and ripped clothing. Bitterly disappointed, we scanned the high city wall that separated us from the mountains of supplies inside. We then saw a spot where the walls had been badly damaged. With great exertion, we scaled the minor · breach with the help of the ropes which we had brought with us to tie up the bundles of supplies that we hoped to get. Once inside, we managed to locate a minor food store where the crush was not so great. Here we managed to bully one of the commissaries into issuing us with a sack of flour, a bag of much-longed-for salt, and some large pieces of salted meat. In another store, which seemed already to have been looted, we fought our way into possession of several pairs of shoes. We left Smolensk over the damaged wall again and made our way back to camp where we all enjoyed the spoils of our perilous exploit.

Next day, our pitifully weak division led the army's retreat. Our halt in

Smolensk meant that the pursuing Russians were now very close behind us. Junot and von Ochs decided to regroup the division into three weak battalions and a 'squadron' of about forty horses to which many mounted officers of all ranks attached themselves. This reorganisation took place at the village of Korytina. General von Ochs commanded the troops; Junot was not to be seen outside his coach.

These paragraphs illustrate two interesting aspects of the retreat at this point. Firstly, the severe degree to which the remnants of the *Grande Armée* had been whittled away so that the VIII Corps was reduced to the equivalent of one of the regiments that had started the campaign; and this was certainly no exception to the now-prevalent rule. Secondly, the Russian high command had no real idea of the scope of this reduction of their enemy's forces. Kutuzov – and all other Russian commanders – were convinced that Napoleon still commanded a strong, fully functional army, and treated him with the respect that such a force demanded. Thus, their pursuit was cautious in the extreme. They had no idea that their strategy had been so destructively successful. They were to remain in ignorance until after the battle of the Beresina Crossing on 26–28 November.

'Next day, we marched on, accompanied by large swarms of unarmed stragglers. A deep silence enveloped the column; we were all sure that we would have a heavy fight with a superior enemy on our hands this day,' continues Morgenstern. It was 15 November.

From 14 to 18 November, the wretched survivors of Napoleon's once-mighty army crawled, clawed, stumbled, and fought their way past part of the Russian army. Miloradovich's 'blocking' force stood respectfully to the south of the road and made little serious attempt to stop the fugitives. Kutuzov came up during the action, but he also was too timid to lock swords seriously with Napoleon, not yet realising how weak his enemy had become. During these five days, over 50,000 survivors of the *Grande Armée* passed through the Russian 'Guard of Honour'. Their losses were estimated by the Russians to be: 13,000 killed, 26,332 captured together with 123 guns, ninety-eight ammunition wagons, fourteen eagle's colours and standards, and Marshal Davout's baton. Kutuzov reported Russian losses as 700 killed and wounded, and was created Prince of Smolensk for the victory. Had the true state of the French been known at this time, it is unlikely that any of them would have escaped. By his timidity, Kutuzov permitted Napoleon and all his generals to slip back to western Europe, thus enabling the war to be carried on through 1813 and 1814.

The Westphalians had managed to get through the potential trap with only light casualties, even though they were marching in battalion squares because of the presence of Russian cavalry. This was due largely to the efforts and initiative of Generals von Ochs and Excelmans, who crewed an abandoned gun by themselves to such good effect that the enemy cavalry stayed at a respectful distance. Junot had attempted to interfere with these two generals at the start of the action, but soon made off in his coach, not to be seen by his command again.

On 17 November, General Count Lambert's advanced guard of Admiral Chichagov's Army of the Danube overran and captured the French magazine in Minsk which held 2 million rations – a severe blow to Napoleon's starving troops. The Russians also captured the 22nd Lithuanian Infantry Regiment and 2000 sick and wounded in the town.

Morgenstern's Division reached Krasnoy in good shape, and took shelter in some abandoned houses, only to be thrown out by force by the Imperial Guard later that night.

Next day, they pushed on towards the Beresina, their numbers dwindling all the time. At Orsha, on the River Dnieper, there was a magazine still functioning, and the Westphalians were able to draw rations. At Bobr, on the river of the same name, their few survivors were reorganised into a single battalion of 400 men.

It was at this time that Admiral Chichagov's Army of the Danube closed up to Borisov, on the River Beresina, perilously close to Napoleon's chosen crossing point. Napoleon was thus about to be caught between two fires and, to make matters worse, the weather conspired against him.

Convinced that he no longer needed his cumbersome bridging train in the bitterly cold Russian winter, on 19 November, the Emperor ordered it burnt at Orsha, using the few remaining horses to pull his guns. Any water obstacle he now had to cross would be frozen solid, thus no longer an obstacle, and could be crossed at any point. Bridges had lost their strategic significance. Luckily, his Chief of Engineers, General Eble, saved some tools and equipment, and had his men carry them on. Just before Napoleon reached the Beresina, a sudden thaw set in, the rivers melted, and bridges – and bridging equipment – became strategically vital again.

On 21 November, Chichagov's advance guard, under General Count Lambert, surprised Dombrowski's 17th Polish Infantry Division at Napoleon's chosen crossing point of Borisov on the Beresina and took the town and the bridgehead. Next day the main body of Chichagov's army also closed up to the town.

On 23 November, the Cossack commander, Count Pahlen, captured two prisoners who told him that the remnants of the *Grande Armée* were only a day's march away from Borisov, and making for that place to cross the Beresina. Chichagov refused to believe the report, took no precautionary measures, and, on 23 November, was bundled out of Borisov with loss by the French as a result. He retreated across the bridge to the fortified bridgehead on the western bank, burning the bridge behind him.

In a masterful stroke, involving deceptive feint attacks and the construction, from materials recovered from the houses of the area, of two rickety bridges over the river between the villages of Brili and Studianka, Napoleon ensured the escape of some of his men from the blundering Russian pursuit. To do it, he sacrificed the newly arrived IX Corps, whose strength fell from 7500 on 27 November to about 1000 after the battle on 28 November.

Total French and allied losses on 27 and 28 November were estimated at 13,000 killed, wounded, and captured as well as four guns and two colours. General Candras was killed; Partouneaux was captured; many generals, including Damas, Fournier, and Girard, were wounded.

After this action the Russian chase slackened. The few survivors of the *Grande Armée* staggered on westwards. Napoleon's great Russian adventure was over; he abandoned the wreck of this army and sped back to Paris to raise another with which to carry on the fight in 1813.

The dramatic year of 1812 was included by Leo Tolstoy in his epic *War and Peace*, as were most of the events in the foregoing pages. Considerable space was devoted to the actual battle of Borodino, to the subsequent burning of Moscow, and to the tragedy of the retreat. Several films have been made of Tolstoy's book, each including extensive coverage of Borodino with more or less convincing footage of what the battle must have been like for the participants. What does not come out in any of these films – or in Tolstoy's book – is the fact that Napoleon's army was practically defeated even before the battle thanks to the strategic errors that he made in advancing as far into Russia as he did in the first place. The significance of Uvarov's raid on the northern flank during the battle is completely overlooked in practically every work.

The Commanders at the Battle
of Borodino

GENERAL PRINCE PIOTR IVANOVICH BAGRATION (1765–1812)

Bagration joined the army in 1782, and was a member of a junior branch of the ruling house of Georgia. He was one of the few survivors of the massacre of Aldee in the Caucasus during the Russo-Turkish war of 1787–91. He served under Suvorov in Poland 1793–94, and in Italy and Switzerland in 1799–1800.

He was highly distinguished at the battles of the Trebbia River (17–20 June 1799) and Novi (15 August 1799), as well as during the crossing of the St Gotthard Pass (23–27 September 1799).

In 1805 Bagration commanded the Austro-Russian rearguard at Schöngraben (16 November) where, with just 5000 men, he held up 30,000 French troops under Murat long enough for the 1st and 2nd Russian armies to effect their junction.

In 1806–07 he again distinguished himself at the battles of Prüssisch-Eylau and Friedland. During the Russo-Swedish war of 1809, he led the famous march across the frozen Gulf of Bothnia.

Commander of the 2nd Army in 1812, he fought like the lion he was despite being profoundly depressed at having to serve under Barclay de Tolly – his junior and a detested foreigner. He was fatally wounded in the violent conflict for the control of the Bagration *flèches* on 7 September at Borodino, and died shortly afterwards. His grave is located at the foot of the monument at the Raevsky Redoubt.

FIELD MARSHAL MIKHAIL BOGDANOVICH BARCLAY DE TOLLY (1761–1818)

Of Scottish and Latvian descent, Barclay de Tolly entered the army in 1776, participated in the Russo-Turkish war (1787–91), the Russo-Swedish war (1783–90), and distinguished himself against Napoleon in 1807 at the battles of Pultusk and Prüssisch-Eylau (wounded). He commanded a corps in the Russo-Swedish war (1808–09), crossing the frozen Straits of Kuarken. From 1810 he was Minister of War. Barclay was the author of the *Yellow Book* that formalised the organisation and planning of the General Staff. In 1812 (initially) he was supreme commander in the west; he saved the Russian armies by clever withdrawal. Barclay de Tolly was superseded on 20 August 1812 by Kutuzov, but continued to command the 1st Army.

Barclay de Tolly displayed great courage at Borodino. He commanded an army in 1813, and was Commander-in-Chief of the Russo-Prussian armies after the battle of Bautzen (20–21 May). He took part in the capture of Paris (30 March 1814) at which he commanded the allied armies. He died in 1818. He was mistrusted and much maligned (quite unjustifiably) by 'real' Russians such as Prince Bagration – himself a Georgian.

LOUIS NICOLAS DAVOUT, MARSHAL OF FRANCE, DUKE OF AUERSTÄDT, PRINCE OF ECKMÜHL (1770–1823)

Described as a dull, stolid, reliable professional, Davout was one of Napoleon's best marshals. He was also in the minority among that group in that he had complete personal integrity.

His father was a junior officer in the cavalry, and Louis Nicolas completed training at the Royal Military School in Paris in 1788 to join his father's regiment. He was an enthusiastic Revolutionary and, by 1791, had been elected lieutenant-colonel commanding his local volunteer battalion. By July 1793 he was promoted Général de Brigade, took a year's sabbatical during the worst of the Terror, and returned to service in late 1794 in command of a cavalry brigade in the Army of the Moselle.

Accompanying Napoleon to Egypt, he fought in several actions including the Pyramids and Aboukir. Attempting to return to France, he was captured by the British and held for a time in Leghorn. After getting to France, he was promoted Général de Division in 1800. By 1801 he was Inspector-General of Cavalry and commanding officer, Foot Grenadiers of the Consular Guard.

He was made Marshal in May 1804, and also became one of the four Colonel-Generals of the Imperial Guard. In 1805, his III Corps won the combat of Mariazell, and played a major part in Napoleon's victory at Austerlitz on 2 December. On 14 October 1806 Davout, with 27,000 men, fought to a standstill the main Prussian army under the aged Duke of Brunswick at Auerstädt while Napoleon defeated another Prussian force at Jena that same day.

Davout was wounded at Eylau (7–8 February 1807) and later became Governor-General of the Grand Duchy of Warsaw. On 24 April 1809, in command of III Corps again, he held out alone in a critical position at Eckmühl. He later fought at Wagram.

In 1812, he commanded the huge I Corps of five divisions; it was a model of good organisation, planning, and discipline. At Borodino it was he who suggested (unsuccessfully) to Napoleon that a strong, southern outflanking move might be decisive.

In 1813, Davout fought at Dresden and Lauenburg, and then defended Hamburg so well that it was not until he received news of Napoleon's abdication in May 1814 that he evacuated the city. He then went into retirement until the Hundred Days when he became Minister for War and Defender of Paris. He capitulated on 3 July 1815 and went into exile. His titles were restored in 1817 and he died in Paris on 1 June 1823.

GENERAL ALEXEI PETROVICH ERMOLOV (1771–1861)

Ermolov entered the army in 1791 having graduated from the Moscow University's Boarding School for Young Noblemen. He served under Suvorov in Poland in 1794. Arrested and exiled during the reign of Tsar Paul I (1796–1801), he was subsequently rehabilitated as commander of a horse artillery battery.

Ermolov distinguished himself at the battles of Austerlitz (2 December 1805) and Prüssisch-Eylau (7–8 February 1807).

He was appointed Chief-of-Staff, 1st Army of the West in 1812 and, by his initiative, saved the Raevsky Battery after it had been stormed by Morand's 1st Division at about 10 a.m. He distinguished himself again in the battle of Malo Jaroslavetz (24 October 1812). In 1813, he commanded the Russo-Prussian rearguard after the battles of Bautzen (20–21 May) and Kulm (30 August). Then, in 1814, Ermolov led a corps of grenadiers in the assault on Paris (30 May). From 1816 to 1827 he was Commander-in-Chief of the Russian troops in Georgia. During the Crimean War (1855) he commanded the Moscow Corps.

PRINCE EUGÈNE DE BEAUHARNAIS, VICEROY OF ITALY (1781–1824)

Born the son of the Vicomte Beauharnais and his wife Josephine Tascher de la Pagerie, Eugène was adopted by Napoleon in 1807, after Napoleon had married Eugène's mother in March 1796. In 1805 he was created Viceroy of the Kingdom of Italy. He was a competent field commander though always terrified of incurring the Emperor's displeasure.

In 1812 he commanded the IV Corps and attached cavalry. During the Battle of Borodino he seemed to panic somewhat at the appearance of Platov's and Uvarov's cavalry on his left flank, and abandoned his assault on the Raevsky Battery, without reference to the Emperor. This action caused a major hiatus in the French offensive, and may well have robbed Napoleon of the crushing victory he so sorely needed.

In 1813 and 1814, Eugène was active in northern Italy against the Austrians (in 1809 he had kept Archduke John out of the main contest at Wagram).

He married the daughter of the King of Bavaria and became Count of Leuchtenberg and Prince of Eichstätt.

EMMANUEL DE GROUCHY, GÉNÉRAL DE DIVISION, COMMANDER, III CAVALRY CORPS (1766–1847)

Of aristocratic descent, Grouchy was the last to be created a marshal by Napoleon (in 1815). By 1786 he was a second lieutenant in the King's Garde du Corps but retired in 1787, having become converted to republican ideals.

He volunteered for service in 1791 and, a year later, was appointed Général de Brigade but was suspended in 1793 because of his aristocratic birth. Reinstated in 1794, he became Général de Division in 1795. Covering the French defeat at Novi on 15 August 1799, he was wounded nine times and captured.

Exchanged in 1800, he transferred to the infantry and distinguished himself at the battle of Hohenlinden on 3 December.

In 1801 he returned to the cavalry. Including those received at Borodino, he was wounded twenty-three times.

He was an abler cavalry commander than Murat, but has been made a scapegoat for Napoleon's defeat at Waterloo in 1815.

MAJOR-GENERAL COUNT ALEXANDER IVANOVICH KUTAISOV (1784–1812)

Kutaisov joined the army in 1805; he distinguished himself at the battle of Prüssisch-Eylau (7–8 February 1807). In 1812 he was commander of the artillery reserve 1st Army. Full of youthful enthusiasm, he joined Ermolov's charge which recaptured the Raevsky Battery at about 10 a.m., and was killed in the process. Control of the 300-gun artillery reserve, and of the ammunition resupply in general, went to pieces after his death because of his inadequate preparations.

FIELD MARSHAL MIKHAIL ILLARIONOVICH KUTUZOV (1745–1813)

Born at St Petersburg on 5 September 1745, Kutuzov was the son of a lieutenant-general who had served under Peter the Great. Kutuzov entered the Russian artillery and engineering school at the age of twelve. Two years later he was posted as a corporal into the artillery. Commissioned at the age of sixteen, he saw active service in Poland from 1764 to 1769, and on the Turkish front from 1770. Distinguished by his great courage on several occasions, he was badly wounded at Shumy in 1774, eventually losing his right eye. He distinguished himself again at the storming of Izmail (also under Suvorov), where he was the first to enter the town. Kutuzov was wounded again at the capture of Okhakov, at the mouth of the Danube, in 1788.

He was promoted Colonel in 1777, Brigadier-General in 1782, and Major-General in 1784.

From 1793 to 1798 he was employed on diplomatic missions. In August 1801 he was relieved of his posts by the new Tsar, Alexander 1, and sent into retirement on suspicion of having been involved in the plot to assassinate Alexander's father, Tsar Paul I.

By 1805, at the outbreak of the war between Austria and France, he was reluctantly rehabilitated and given command of the Russian army that hurried – too late – to Austria's aid. Alexander I rejected Kutuzov's plans for the operations around Austerlitz (2 December 1805) which led to a crushing Austro-Russian defeat. Kutuzov became the imperial whipping boy.

By 1811 he was again on the Turkish frontier, charged with ending the conflict there to release Russian forces to come north to defend the Fatherland against Napoleon. He succeeded.

On 20 August 1812 Tsar Alexander confirmed Kutuzov as Supremo, on the recommendation of the Emergency Committee.

In 1813, on the advance through Saxony, Kutuzov fell ill at Bunzlau and died on 28 April. His remains were interred in the Kazan Cathedral in St Petersburg on 25 June 1812.

MAJOR-GENERAL PIOTR GAVRILOVICH LIKHACHEV (1758–1812)

Likhachev joined the army in 1773 and was made up to second-lieutenant in 1779. He served under Suvorov in the Trans-Kuban campaign of 1783, and in the Russo-Swedish war of 1788–90. From 1797 he served in the Caucasus. In 1809 he was appointed chief of the Tomsk Musketeer

Regiment; in 1812, Commander 24th Infantry Division, in Dokhturov's VI Corps.

Likhachev fought at Smolensk.

Towards the end of the battle of Borodino, the 24th Division took over the defence of the Raevsky Battery. Likhachev was wounded several times and captured in the final assault by Prince Eugène's troops at about 3 p.m. He was captured and sent to Prussia but died there (in Königsberg) on the way to France.

GENERAL DMITRI PETROVICH NEVEROVSKY (1771–1813)

In 1804 Neverovsky commanded a regiment of marines and in 1807 the Pavlov Grenadiers. In 1812 he commanded the newly formed 27th Division which acquitted itself so well on 14 August at Krasnoy where it held its own against double its numbers of Marshal Ney's cavalry.

In 1813 he was killed during the Battle of Leipzig (16–19 October).

COUNT MATVEI IVANOVICH PLATOV, ATAMAN OF THE DON COSSACKS (1751–1818)

Platov was a young commander of his own Cossack Pulk (regiment), and was promoted Major-General for his conduct in the capture of Izmail from the Turks in 1790.

During the reign of Tsar Paul I (1796–1801), he fell into disgrace and was initially imprisoned in the notorious Peter and Paul Fortress in St Petersburg. Later he was exiled to the Kostroma region of Siberia.

When Alexander came to the throne, he was rehabilitated and took part in the abortive expedition to India. Later promoted to Lieutenant-General, he was appointed Ataman (Head Man) of the Don Cossacks.

He served in the 1806–07 campaign against Napoleon, and then on the lower Danube in 1808–09 against the Turks. His Cossacks became the terror of Napoleon's *Grande Armée* in 1812, and it was his suggestion that led to Uvarov's raid during the battle of Borodino. He was active during the 1813 and 1814 campaigns, and died in 1818.

GENERAL NIKOLAI NIKOLAIEVICH RAEVSKY
(1771–1829)

Commissioned in 1786, Raevsky fought against the Turks 1788–90 and in Poland under Suvorov 1792–94. He commanded the Nizhin-Novgorod Dragoons in 1796. He fought in the war against France in 1806–07 and in the Russo-Swedish war of 1809. In 1810 he was employed against the Turks on the lower Danube. At the beginning of 1812 he was Commander VII Infantry Corps in Bagration's 2nd Army. He distinguished himself in the combat of Saltanovka (23 July), the battle of Smolensk (17–18 August), and at Borodino in the tenacious defence of the battery that carried his name.

During 1813 and 1814, Raevsky fought at Bautzen, Dresden, and Leipzig, and in the capture of Paris. He retired in 1824.

The Orders of Battle

THE *GRANDE ARMÉE*

On the right-hand side of the page, in brackets, are shown the officer casualties incurred by each regiment on 7 September. Those killed and mortally wounded are shown before the oblique stroke; those wounded are shown after it. These data are taken from; *Tableaux par Corps et par Batailles des Officiers Tués et Blessés Pendant les Guerres de l'Empire (1805–1815)* by A. Martinien.

Napoleon I
Imperial Headquarters

Chief-of-Staff: Marshal Alexander Berthier
Commander of the Cavalry: Joachim Murat, King of Naples
Commander of the Artillery: General Laribossière
Commander of the Engineers: General Chasseloup

Other staff personnel consisted of about twenty generals and 400 other officers.

Imperial Headquarters escort: Gendarmerie d'Elite	2 squadrons
7e Chasseurs à Cheval	4 squadrons

The Imperial Guard
The Old Guard: Marshal Lefebvre, Duke of Danzig

1st Division: General Delaborde

General Berthezène	4e Tirailleurs	2 bns
	4e Voltigeurs	2 bns
	5e Voltigeurs	2 bns (-/1)
General Lanusse	5e Tirailleurs	2 bns
	6e Tirailleurs	2 bns
	6e Voltigeurs	2 bns

3rd Division: General Curial

General Boyer	1er Chasseurs à Pied	2 bns
	2e Chasseurs à Pied	2 bns

	1er Grenadiers	2 bns
	2e Grenadiers	2 bns
	3e Grenadiers	2 bns

The Young Guard: Marshal Mortier, Duke of Treviso
General Roguet

General Lanabèze	1er Voltigeurs	2 bns
	1er Tirailleurs	2 bns (-/1)
General Boyledieu	Fusilier-Chasseurs	2 bns
	Fusilier-Grenadiers	2 bns

The Legion of the Vistula: General Claparède

General Chlopicki	1st Infantry Regiment	3 bns
	2nd Infantry Regiment	3 bns
General Bronikowski	3rd Infantry Regiment	3 bns
	4th Infantry Regiment	3 bns

The Guard Cavalry: Marshal Bessières

1st Brigade, General	Dragoons	4 sqns (-/1)
St Sulpice	Grenadiers à Cheval	4 sqns
2nd Brigade, General Guyot	Chasseurs à Cheval	4 sqns
	Mamelukes	1 sqn
3rd Brigade, General Colbert	1er (Polish) Ch. L. L.	4 sqns
	2e (Dutch) Ch. L. L.	4 sqns (1/-)

Other attached troops:

Chasseurs à Cheval of the Portuguese Legion	3 sqns
Velites of Prince Borghese	1 bn
Velites of the Italian Guard	1 bn
2nd Infantry Regiment of Baden	2 bns

Guard Artillery: General Sorbier (each of the infantry regiments shown above had its own integral artillery section of two guns).

The Old Guard	2 batteries
The Young Guard	1 battery
The Artillery Park	3 HA batteries
	4 foot batteries
Sappers	2 companies
Train	14 companies
Artificers	2 companies

I Infantry Corps: Marshal Davout, Prince of Eckmühl

1st Division: General Morand

General D'Alton	13e Légère	5 bns (7/20)
General Gratien	17e Ligne	5 bns (26/28)
General Bonamy	30e Ligne	5 bns (22/30)

Artillery: 1 foot, 1 HA battery, 2 train companies, 1 company of
sappers, 1 company of equipment train
2nd Division: General Friant

General Dufour	15e Légère	5 bns (10/30)
General Vandedem	33e Ligne	5 bns (9/19)
General Grandeau	48e Ligne	5 bns (9/22)
	Spanish Regiment Joseph	
	Napoleon	2 bns

Artillery: 1 foot, 1 HA battery, 2 train companies,
1 company of sappers, 1 company of equipment train
3rd Division: General Gérard

	7e Légère	5 bns (7/17)
General Desailly	12e Ligne	5 bns (7/18)
General Leclerc	21e Ligne	5 bns (6/22)

Artillery: 1 foot, 1 HA battery, 2 train companies,
1 company of sappers, 2 companies of equipment
train
4th Division: General Desaix

| General Fréderichs | 85e Ligne | 5 bns (6/10) |
| General Leguay | 108e Ligne | 5 bns (2/13) |

Artillery:1 foot, 1 HA battery, 2 train companies,
1 company of sappers, 1 company of equipment train
5th Division: General Compans

General Duppelin	25e Ligne	5 bns (3/6)
	includes Shevardino	
General Teste	57e Ligne	5 bns (14/26)
General Goyordet	61e Ligne	5 bns (6/13)
Colonel Juillet	111e Ligne	5 bns (7/20)

Artillery: 1 foot, 1 HA battery, 2 train companies,
1 company of sappers, 1 company of equipment train
Attached Light Cavalry
1st Brigade, General Pajol

| | 2e Ch.-à-Ch. | 4 sqns (2/3) |
| | 9th Polish Lancers | 4 sqns (-/7) |

2nd Brigade, General Bourdesoul

| | 1e Ch.-à-Ch. | 4 sqns (2/8) |
| | 3e Ch.-à-Ch. | 4 sqns (2/5) |

Reserve Artillery of the I Corps: General Pernety
5 foot artillery batteries, 5 train companies, 1 artificer company

III Infantry Corps: Marshal Ney, Duke of Elchingen

10th Division: General Ledru

Genernal Gengoult	24e Légère	4 bns (8/7)
Colonel Pego	Portuguese Legion	
	1st Infantry Regiment	2 bns (5/9)
General Morion	46e Ligne	4 bns (5/12)
General Bruny	72e Ligne	4 bns (15/14)

Artillery: 1 foot, 1 HA battery, 2 train companies,
1 sapper company, 1 company of equipment train

11th Division: General Razout

General Joubert	4e Ligne	4 bns (9/22)
General Compère	18e Ligne	4 bns (11/30)
Colonel Xavier	Portuguese Legion	
	2nd Infantry Regiment	2 bns (9/12)
General D'Henin	93e Ligne	4 bns (4/18)

Artillery: 1 foot, 1 HA battery, 2 train companies,
1 sapper company, 1 equipment train company

*25th (Württemberg) Division: French Lieutenant General Count Marchand,
General Baron Ernst von Hügel, Colonel von Stockmeyer*

1st Provisional Bn	1 bn
2nd Provisional Bn	1 bn [1st and 2nd (1/9)]
3rd Provisional (Light) Bn	1 bn (3/4)

Artillery: 1 foot, 1 HA battery, 2 train companies, 1 sapper company,
1 equipment train company

Attached Light Cavalry

9th Brigade, General Mouriez

	11e Hussars	4 sqns (1/8)
	6e Chevaux-légèrs	4 sqns (3/8)
4th (Württemberg)		
	Jaeger-zu-Pferde	4 sqns (2/6)

14th (Württemberg) Brigade: General Beurmann

	4e (French) Ch.-à-Ch.	4 sqns (2/5)
	1st Chevaux-légèrs	4 sqns (1/8)
	2nd Chevaux-légèrs	4 sqns (1/5)
	3rd Jaeger-zu-Pferde	3 sqns (3/4)

III Corps Artillery: General Foucher

3 French foot batteries, 2 Württemberg foot batteries, 2 French and 1
Württemberg HA batteries, 6 train companies, 1 sapper company, 1
equipment train company

IV Infantry Corps: Prince Eugène, Viceroy of Italy

The Italian Royal Guard: General Lecchi

Colonel Bataglia	Gardes d'Honneur	5 coys
Major Crovi	Infantry Regiment	2 bns
Colonel Peraldi	Conscript Regiment	2 bns
	Marines	1 coy

Cavalry: General Triaire

Colonel Jaquet	Dragoons	4 sqns
Colonel Narboni	Dragoni Regina	4 sqns

Artillery of the Italian Guard: 1 foot, 1 HA battery,
2 companies of artillery train, 1 company of artificers,
1 sapper company, 2 companies of equipment
train

13th Division: General Delzon

General Huard	8e Légère	2 bns
	84e Ligne	4 bns
General Roussel	92e Ligne	4 bns (-/8)
Colonel Slivarich	1st Croatian Inf. Regt	2 bns
General Guyon	106e Ligne	4 bns (18/32)

Artillery: 1 foot, 1 HA battery, 2 companies artillery train,
1 sapper company, 1 artificer company, 1 equipment
train company

14th Division: General Broussier

General de Sivray	18e Légère	2 bns (-/2)
	9e Ligne	4 bns (8/36)
General Alméras	35e Ligne	4 bns (4/15)
Major Doreille	Spanish Inf. Regt.	
	Joseph Napoleon	2 bns (2/5)
General Pastol	53e Ligne	4 bns (4/21)

Artillery: 1 foot, 1 HA battery, 2 companies artillery train, 1 sapper
company, 1 artificer company, 1 equipment train company

15th (Italian) Division: General Pinot (reached the battlefield
only at 9 o'clock that night)

	1st Light Inf. Regt	1 bn
	3rd Light Inf. Regt	4 bns
	2nd Line Inf. Regt	4 bns
	3rd Line Inf. Regt	4 bns
	Dalmatian Inf. Regt	3 bns

Artillery: 1 foot, 1 HA battery, 2 companies artillery train,
1 sapper company, 1 artificer company, 1 equipment
train company

Attached Light Cavalry: General Omano
12th Light Cavalry Brigade: General Ferrière

9e Ch.-à-Ch.	4 sqns (1/6)
19e Ch.-à-Ch.	4 sqns (-/6)

13th Light Cavalry Brigade: General Villata

2nd (Italian) Ch.-à-Ch.	4 sqns
3rd (Italian) Ch.-à-Ch.	4 sqns

1st (Bavarian) Light Cavalry Brigade: General Count von Seydewitz

3rd Bavarian Chevaux-légèrs Regt	4 sqns (-/6)
6th Bavarian Chevaux-légèrs Regt	4 sqns (-/5)

22nd (Bavarian) Light Cavalry Brigade: General Preysing

4th Bavarian Chevaux-légèrs Regt	4 sqns (1/4)
5th Bavarian Chevaux-légèrs Regt	4 sqns (1/4)

Artillery: 4 foot batteries, 4 train companies, 1 sapper company, 2 pontonnier companies, 1 artificer company, 1 engineer train company

The V (Polish) Infantry Corps: General Prince Poniatowski

16th Division: General Zayonczek

General Mielzynski	3rd Inf. Regt	3 bns (4/8)
	15th Inf. Regt	3 bns (3/8)
General Poszhowski	16th Inf. Regt	3 bns (2/6)

Artillery: 2 foot batteries, 2 train companies, 1 sapper company, 1 'supplementary' company, 7 artificers

18th Division: General Kniaziewicz

General Grabowski	2nd Inf. Regt	3 bns (2/6)
	8th Inf. Regt	3 bns (2/10)
General Wierzbinski	12th Inf. Regt	3 bns (3/10)

Artillery: 2 foot batteries, 2 train companies, 1 sapper company, 1 'supplementary' company, 7 artificiers

Attached Light Cavalry
18th (Polish) Light Cavalry Brigade: General Niemojewski

4th Ch.-à-Ch.	4 sqns (1/5)

19th (Polish) Light Cavalry Brigade: General Tyskiewicz

1st Ch.-à-Ch.	1 sqn
12th Lancers	4 sqns (1/6)

5th (Polish) Light Cavalry Brigade: General Prince Sulkowski

5th Ch.-à-Ch.	4 sqns (1/7)
13th Hussars	4 sqns (-/9)

V Corps Artillery Reserve
1 HA battery, 6 foot batteries, 8 train companies, 2 'supplementary' companies, ½ a company of artificers, 1 company of sappers, 1 company of pontonniers, 1 battalion of 'Equipages Militaires'

The VIII (Westphalian) Infantry Corps: General Junot,
Duke of Abrantes

23rd Division: General Tharreau
1st Brigade: General Damas

	3rd Light Bn	1 bn. (-/5)
	2nd Line Inf. Regt	2 bns (3/8)
	6th Line Inf. Regt	2 bns (2/7)

2nd Brigade: General von Borstell

	2nd Light Bn	1 bn. (-/8)
	3rd Line Inf. Regt	2 bns (-/9)
	7th Line Inf. Regt	3 bns (2/12)

Artillery: 1 foot battery, 1 train company
24th Division: General von Ochs
1st Brigade: General Legras

	Jaeger-Carabiniers	1 bn (-/6)
	Gardes-Jaegers	1 bn (-/5)
	Gardes-Grenadières	1 bn (1/4)
	1st Light Bn	1 bn (-/7)

Artillery: 1 foot, 1 HA battery, 2 train companies
Attached Light Cavalry
24th (Westphalian) Light Cavalry Brigade: General von Hammerstein

	1st Hussars	4 sqns (1/16)
	2nd Hussars	4 sqns (3/14)
General von Wolf	Garde Chevaux-légèrs	
	Regt	4 sqns (1/9)

VIII Corps Artillery Reserve
2 foot batteries, 2 train companies, 1 sapper company, ½ a company of artificers

I Reserve Cavalry Corps: General Nansouty

1st Light Cavalry Division: General Bruyère
3rd Light Cavalry Brigade: General Jacquinot

	7e Hussars	4 sqns (1/5)
	9e Chevaux-légèrs	4 sqns (-/14)

4th Light Cavalry Brigade: General Piré

	8e Hussars	4 sqns (1/1)
	16e Ch.-à-Ch.	4 sqns (1/6)

15th Light Cavalry Brigade: General Niewiewski

	6th (Polish) Lancers	4 sqns (1/8)
	8th (Polish) Lancers	4 sqns (1/5)
	2nd (Prussian) Hussars	4 sqns (1/3)

Artillery: 1 HA battery, 1 train company

1st Cuirassier Division: General Saint-Germain
1st Brigade: General Bessières

2e Cuirassiers	4 sqns (1/8)

2nd Brigade: General Bruno

3e Cuirassiers	4 sqns (1/7)

3rd Brigade: General Quenot

9e Cuirassiers	4 sqns (3/9)
1er Chevaux-légèrs	4 sqns (-/3)

Artillery: 2 HA batteries, 2 train companies
5th Cuirassier Division: General Valence
1st Brigade: General Reynaud.

6e Cuirassiers	4 sqns (-/5)

2nd Brigade: General Dejean

11e Cuirassiers	4 sqns (1/3)

3rd Brigade: General Delagrange

12e Cuirassiers	4 sqns (-/7)
5e Chevaux-légèrs	4 sqns (-/3)

Artillery: 2 HA batteries, 2 train companies

II Reserve Cavalry Corps: General Montbrun
2nd Light Cavalry Division: General Sebastiani
7th Light Brigade: General Saint-Génies

11e Chasseurs	4 sqns (1/7)
12e Chasseurs	4 sqns (6/11)

8th Brigade: General Baurth

5e Hussars	4 sqns (2/11)
9e Hussars	4 sqns (2/5)

16th Brigade: General Suberwiecz

1st Prussian Ulans	4 sqns (1/3)
3rd Württemberg Jaeger-zu-Pferde	4 sqns (-/1)
10th Polish Hussars	4 sqns (1/8)

2nd Cuirassier Division: General Wathier
1st and 2nd Brigades: General Caulaincourt

5e Cuirassiers	4 sqns (1/9)
8e Cuirassiers	4 sqns (4/12)

3rd Brigade: General Richter

10e Cuirassiers	4 sqns (1/4)
2e Chasseurs	4 sqns (2/3)

Artillery: 2 HA batteries, 2 train companies
4th Cuirassier Division: General Defrance
1st Brigade: General Berkheim

1er Carabiniers	4 sqns (3/8)

2nd Brigade: General L'Eritage

2e Carabiniers	4 sqns (2/7)

3rd Brigade: General Ornano (detached to IV Corps)

1er Cuirassiers	4 sqns (-/3)
4e Chevaux-légèrs	4 sqns (1/3)

Artillery: 2 HA batteries, 2 train companies

III Reserve Cavalry Corps: General Grouchy

3rd Light Cavalry Division: General Chastel
10th Brigade: General Gauthrin

6e Chasseurs	4 sqns (1/11)
8e Chasseurs	4 sqns (-/6)

11th Brigade: General Gérard

6e Hussars	4 sqns (2/7)
25e Chasseurs	4 sqns (-/15)

17th Brigade, General Domanget

1st Bavarian Chevaux-légèrs	4 sqns (4/13)
2nd Bavarian Chevaux-légèrs	4 sqns (2/7)
Saxon Chevaux-légèrs 'Prinz Albrecht'	4 sqns (4/5)

6th Heavy Cavalry Division: General La Haussaye
1st Brigade: General Thiry

7e Dragons	4 sqns (1/13)
23e Dragons	4 sqns (2/5)

2nd Brigade: General Seron

28e Dragons	4 sqns (2/9)
30e Dragons	4 sqns (1/9)

Artillery: 2 HA batteries, 2 train companies

IV Reserve Cavalry Corps: General Latour-Maubourg

4th (Polish) Light Cavalry Division: General Rozniecki
29th Brigade: General Turno

3rd Lancers	4 sqns (6/10)
11th Lancers	3 sqns (3/17)
16th Lancers	4 sqns (2/10)

Artillery: 2 HA batteries, 2 train companies
7th Cuirassier Division: General Lorge
1st Brigade: General Thielemann

Saxon Garde du Corps	4 sqns (8/10)
Saxon Cuirassier Regiment	
von Zastrow	4 sqns (10/8)
14th Polish Cuirassiers	4 sqns (2/9)

2nd Brigade: General Lepel

1st Westphalian Cuirassiers	4 sqns (2/7)
2nd Westphalian Cuirassiers	4 sqns (1/8)

Artillery: 2 HA batteries, 2 train companies

The officer losses suffered by the *Grande Armée* in the struggle for the Shevardino Redoubt on 5 September are recorded in Martinien as follows:

1st Division: 17 Ligne – 4/7

5th Division: 25e Ligne – losses shown combined with those of 7 September

57e Ligne – 6/6

61e Ligne – -/4

111e Ligne – 3/5

13th Division: 84e Ligne – -/1

9th Light Cavalry Brigade, III Corps: 11e Hussars – 2/9

THE RUSSIAN ARMY

(after Bogdanovich)

Commander-in-Chief: General-of-Infantry Prince Mikhail
Illarionovich Golenishchev Kutuzov
Chief-of-Staff: General-of-Cavalry Count Bennigsen; Colonel von Toll
Aide-du-Jour: Colonel Kaiserov
Quartermaster-General: Major-General Vistitski II
Commander of Engineers: Major-General Ivachev

Headquarters Guard:

2nd Combined Grenadier Battalion; Selenginsk Infantry Regiment (1
bn); Kargopol Dragoons (4 sqns); Ingermanland Dragoons (4 sqns); 2nd
Bug Cossack Regiment; engineers (3 companies).
Unless otherwise noted, all infantry regiments have two battalions.

Under command of General-of-Infantry Barclay de Tolly, 1st Army of
the West
Chief-of-Staff: General Ermolof
Commander of the Artillery: Major-General Count Kutaisov (see
below)
Commander of Engineers: Major-General Truson

The Right Wing: General-of-Infantry Miloradovich

II Infantry Corps: Lieutenant-General Baggovut
4th Infantry Division: Major-General Duke Eugen von Württemberg
Infantry Regiments: Tobolsk, Volhynia, Kremenchug, Minsk, 4th and
34th Jaegers, Position Battery Nr 4
17th Infantry Division: Lieutenant-General Alsufevev
Infantry Regiments: Ryazan, Belozersk, Brest, Willmanstrand, 30th
and 48th Jaegers, Position Battery Nr17

Total II Corps: 24 battalions; 2 batteries; 10,300 men; 24 guns

IV Infantry Corps: Lieutenant-General Count Ostermann-Tolstoy
11th Infantry Division: Major-General Bakhmetiev II
Infantry Regiments: Kexholm, Pernau, Polotsk, Elets, 1st and 33rd
Jaegers, Combined Grenadier Regiment, Position Battery Nr 11

23rd Infantry Division: Major-General Bakhmetiev I
Infantry Regiments: Rylsk, Ekaterinburg, Selenginsk, 18th Jaegers,

one Combined Grenadier Battalion, Light Battery Nr 44

Total IV Corps: 23 battalions; 2 batteries; 9500 men; 24 guns

I Cavalry Corps: General-Adjutant Uvarov
Life Guard Dragoons, Life Guard Hussars, Life Guard Ulans, Life
Guard Cossacks, Nizhin Dragoons (4 squadrons each), Elisabetgrad
Hussars (8 squadrons), Horse Artillery Battery Nr 5

Total I Cavalry Corps: 28 squadrons; 1 battery; 2500 men; 12 guns

II Cavalry Corps: General-Adjutant Baron Korf
Dragoon Regiments Pskov, Moscow, Kargopol, Ingermanland (4
squadrons each), Polish Ulan Regiment, Sumy Hussars (8 squadrons
each), Horse Artillery Battery Nr 4

Total II Cavalry Corps: 32 squadrons; 1 battery; 3500 men; 12
guns

The Centre: General-of-Infantry Dokhturov
VI Infantry Corps: General-of-Infantry Dokhturov
7th Infantry Division: Lieutenant-General Kaptsevich
Infantry Regiments: Moscow, Pskov, Sofia, Libau, 11th and 36th
Jaegers, Combined Grenadier Regiment, Position Battery Nr 7

24th Infantry Division, Major-General Likhachev
Infantry Regiments: Ufimsk, Shirvan, Butyrsk, Tomsk, 19th and
40th Jaegers, Combined Grenadier Regiment, Position Battery
Nr 24

Total VI Infantry Corps: 28 battalions: 2 batteries; 9900 men; 24
guns

III Cavalry Corps: (owing to the sickness of Lieutenant-General
Count Pahlen, this formation was commanded by General-Adjutant
Baron Korf)
Major-General Kreutz: Dragoon Regiments Courland, Orenburg,
Siberia, Irkutsk (4 squadrons each); Hussar Regiments Sumy, Mariupol
(8 squadrons each); Horse Artillery Battery Nr 9

Total III Cavalry Corps: 32 squadrons; 1 battery; 3700 men, 12
guns

The Reserve of the Right Wing and the Centre
V Infantry Corps: Lieutenant-General Lavrov

Life Guard Regiments: Preobrazhensky, Semenovsky, Lithuania, Finland, and Jaegers (3 battalions each); Guards Marine Equipage (1 battalion); Combined Grenadier Battalions of the 4th Division, 17th Division, 1st Division, and 3rd Division (2 battalions each)

Total V Infantry Corps: 27 battalions; 13,000 men
1st Cuirassier Division: Major-General Borozdin II
Chevalier Guards, Life Horse Guards, Cuirassier Regiments His Majesty, Her Majesty, and Astrakhan (4 squadrons each)

Total 1st Cuirassier Division: 20 squadrons; 2,400 men

Reserve Artillery: Major-General Count Kutaizov, then Major-General Löwenstern and Colonel Eiler: Guards Artillery Brigade (6 batteries), 6 Position Batteries, 9 light batteries, 5 horse artillery batteries, 1 pionier and 2 pontonnier companies

Total Artillery Reserve: 8400 men; 26 batteries; 300 guns (the 2 horse artillery batteries of the Guard had 8 guns each, the 1st Light Battery of the Guard included 2 guns of the Marine Equipage)

The Left Wing: General-of-Infantry Prince Bagration
Lieutenant-Generals Prince Gorchakov II and Prince Golytsin
VII Infantry Corps: Lieutenant-General Raevsky
26th Infantry Division: Major-General Paskevich
Infantry Regiments: Ladoga, Poltava, Nizhegorod, Orel, 5th and 42nd Jaegers, Position Battery Nr 26, Light Battery Nr 47
12th Infantry Division: Major-General Vasil'chikov
Infantry Regiments: Narva, Smolensk, New Ingermanland, 6th and 41st Jaegers

Total VII Infantry Corps: 24 battalions; 2 batteries; 10,800 men; 24 guns

VIII Infantry Corps: Lieutenant-General Borozdin II
2nd Grenadier Division: Major-General Prince Karl von Mecklenburg
Grenadier Regiments: Kiev, Astrakhan, Moscow, Phanagoria, Siberia, and Little Russia; Position Battery Nr 2; Light Battery Nr 3
27th Infantry Division: Major-General Neverovsky

Infantry Regiments: Vilensk, Simbirsk, Odessa, Tarnopol, 49th and 50th Jaegers

Total VIII Infantry Corps: 24 battalions; 2 batteries; 11,200 men; and 24 guns

IV Cavalry Corps: Major-General Count Siever I
Dragoon Regiments: Kharkov, Chernigov, Kiev, New Russia (4 squadrons each); Hussar Regiment Akhtyrka, Lithuanian Ulan Regiment (8 squadrons each); Horse Artillery Battery Nr 10

Total IV Cavalry Corps: 32 squadrons; 1 battery; 3800 men; 12 guns

Reserve of the Left Wing

2nd Combined Grenadier Division: Major-General Count Vorontsov
The Combined Grenadier Regiments of the 2nd, 12th, and 26th Divisions (2 battalions each). Total: 2100 men

The Combined Grenadier Regiments of the 7th and 24th Divisions were deployed as supports for the Jaegers who were in skirmishing order along the front.

2nd Cuirassier Division: Major-General Duka
Cuirassier Regiments: Ekaterinoslav, Military Order, Glukhov, Little Russia, and Novgorod. Total: 20 squadrons; 2300 men

Reserve Artillery of the Left Wing: seven batteries, one pionier, and one pontonnier company. Total: 2400 men; 84 guns

On the Old Smolensk Road, III Infantry Corps: Lieutenant-General Tuchkov I
1st Grenadier Division: Major-General Stroganov
Grenadier Regiments: Life Guards, Arakcheev, Pavlov, St Petersburg, Ekaterinoslav, Tavrichesk (2 battalions each); Position Battery Nr 1; Light Batteries Nr 1 and 2

3rd Infantry Division: Lieutenant-General Konovnitsyn.
Infantry Regiments: Muromsk, Revel, Chernigov, Kaporie; 20th and 21st Jaegers; Position Battery Nr 3; Light Batteries Nr 5 and 6

Total: 24 battalions; 6 batteries; 8000 men; 72 guns

Cossacks: Major-General Karpov: 6 regiments, 1500 men

Moscow Militia: Lieutenant-General Count Markov
Smolensk Militia: Lieutenant-General Lebedev

Total Militia:10,000 men

Total of the Russian Army: 180 battalions; 164 squadrons; 55 batteries; 2 pionier and 3 pontonnier companies: with a strength of 103,800 men, 640 guns, plus 7000 Cossacks and 10,000 militia

N.B. A Position Battery had 12-pounder guns, Light and Horse Artillery Batteries used 6-pounders.

Russian losses according to some of the monuments on the field

27th Infantry Division Killed, Wounded, and Missing

Regiment	Officers	Men
Vilnius	18	345
Simbirsk	18	969
Odessa	21	491
Tarnopol	30	750
Totals	87	2,280

2nd Grenadier Division Killed, Wounded and Missing

Regiment	Officers	Men
Kiev	17	272
Moscow	23	658
Siberia	13	468
Little Russia	21	692
Phanagoria	34	493
Astrakhan	36	932
Totals	144	3,515

4th Infantry Division

	Officers	Men
Killed	7	520
Wounded	13	515
Totals	20	1,035

24th Infantry Division

Officers	Men
23	527
20	621
43	1,148

IV Cavalry Corps
Dragoons killed, wounded and missing all shown together

Regiment	Officers (Killed)	Men (Killed)	Officers (Wounded)	Men (Wounded)	Missing
Kharkov	5	9	6	35	–
Chernigov	1	42	12	84	16
Kiev	4	?	7	526★	?
New Russia	3	100	5	?	?
Arkhangelsk Hussars	2	29	13	110	?
Totals	15	180	3	791	?

Killed, Wounded, and Missing

Astrakhan Cuirassiers: Parade state, morning, 7 September 563 all ranks
Killed, wounded, and missing 468
Survivors 95

Guard Jaegers: Parade state, morning, 7 September 51 officers, 1834
men
Killed, wounded, and missing 27 officers, 693 men

1st Guards Horse Artillery Battery (8 guns)
Parade state, morning, 7 September 9 officers, 195 men

	Officers	Men
Killed	2	12
Wounded	1	46
Total losses	3	58

Guards Marine Equipage Parade state, morning, 7 September 1 officer,
30 men

	Officers	Men
Killed, wounded, and missing	11	

THE BORODINO MONUMENTS

The battlefield is covered with monuments to various individuals, regiments, divisions, and corps; the following list will serve to give an overview of them and an idea of where to find some of them.

The information is taken from a small, tourist map, on sale at the battlefield shop today. The map is reproduced in the booklet, *Borodino Fotoputevoditel* (Moscow, Planeta Press, 1991).

1	Shevardino Redoubt. In the redoubt is a monument to the 12th Artillery Battery.
2	The Raevsky Battery.
3	The lower Gorki Battery.
4	The upper Gorki Battery.
5	The Maslovsky Battery (in the woods NE of Gorki).
6	The Kryushinsky Battery (NE of Gorki)
7	The site of the Russian HQ on the day of the battle (S of Gorki).
8	Site of the Russian General Staff on the day of the battle (E of Gorki).
9	Site of French 'Bogarny' Battery (W of Borodino).
10	Site of the French 'Fouche' Battery (E of Shevardino).
11	Site of French 'Sorbier' Battery (E of Shevardino).
12	Grave of Captain A. G. Ogarev, Finland Lifeguards Regiment (SE of Semenovskaya).
13	Grave of the Unknown Soldier (by the northernmost Bagration *flèche*).
14	Grave of General D. L. Neverovsky (in the southernmost Bagration *flèche*).
15 & 16	Graves of Russian soldiers in Utitsa wood (south of the southern Bagration *flèche*).
17	Grave of Prince Bagration [at the foot of the main monument to the battle, on the site of the Raevsky Battery (49)].
18	Grave of Russian officers (E of Utitsa).
19	1st Grenadier Division, III Corps (ESE of the Bagration *flèches*).
20	17th Division, II Corps (E of Utitsa).
21	Pavlovsky Grenadier Regiment (ESE of the Bagration *flèches*).
22	Moscow and Smolensk Militia (E of the Bagration *flèches*).
23 & 24	Lithuanian Lifeguards (NE of Semenovskaya).
25	Finland Lifeguards (in Semenovskaya).
26	2nd Cuirassier Division (W of Semenovskaya).
27	Izmail Lifeguards (SW of Semenovskaya).
28	Lifeguards Artillery Brigade (W of Semenovskaya).
29	2nd Battery, Lifeguards Artillery Brigade (W of Semenovskaya).
30	IV Cavalry Corps (W of the Bagration *flèches*).
31	Muromsk Infantry Regiment (S of the Bagration *flèches*).
32	2nd Grenadier Division (S of the Bagration *flèches*).

33	3rd Infantry Division (SW of Semenovskaya).
34	27th Infantry Division (S of the Bagration *flèches*).
35	Pioniers (in the Shevardino Redoubt).
36	4th Infantry Division (N of Semenovskaya).
37	1st Horse Artillery Battery, Lifeguards Artillery Brigade, Captain P. I. Zakharov (W of the Raevsky Battery).
38	III Cavalry Corps (between the Raevsky Battery and Semenovskaya).
39	Site of twelve French batteries (W of Semenovskaya).
40	Volhynia Infantry Regiment (at the confluence of the Kolocha and the Stonets streams).
41	12th Infantry Division (south of the Bagration *flèches*).
42	24th Infantry Division.
43	The main Russian Army monument (in the Raevsky Battery).
44	Nizhin Dragoon Regiment (N of Borodino).
45	I Cavalry Corps (N of Borodino).
46	Ataman Platov's Don Cossacks (north of Borodino).
47	Lifeguard Jaegers and Guards Marine Equipage (W of Gorki).
48	1st and 19th Jaegers (W of Gorki).
49	Lifeguard Cossacks.
50	7th Infantry Division, General P. M. Kaptsevich.
51	Chevalier Guards and Horse Guards (E of Raevsky Battery).
52	Astrakhan Cuirassier Regiment.
53	23rd Infantry Division.
54	Monument to the *Grande Armée* (NE of the Shevardino Redoubt).
55	Red Army monument (T34 tank, W of Raevsky Battery).
56	The museum of the Battle of Borodino 1812 (W of the Raevsky Battery).

OVERVIEW OF THE ACTIONS ON THE VARIOUS FRONTS

	Latvia	North	Centre	South
July		9 Korelichi		
			10 Mir	
			15 Romanovo	
19	Eckau			
			23 Saltanovka	
			27 Ostrovno	27 Kobryn
		28 Kliastitsy	28 Akubovo	
		30 Kliastitsy		
August				
		2 Golovchichtsy		
5	Schlock			
7	Volgund			
				8 Rudnia
		11 Svolna		
				12 Gorodetsna
			14 Krasnoy	
		16–18 1st Polotsk		
			17–18 Smolensk	
			19 Valutina Gora	
22	Dahlenkirchen, Olai, Schlock			
September				
			5 Shevardino	
			7 Borodino	
			10 Mozhaisk	
				20 Neskhviz
27	Eckau			
29	Mesoten			29 Luboml
30	Lautschkruge, Graefenthal			
October				
1	Garosse River		11 Trycziner Hof	
				13 Biala Podlaska
		18–20 2nd Polotsk	18 Vinkovo	
			20 Slonim	
			24 Maloyaroslavets	
		31 Chashniky		
November				
			3 Viasma	
		7 Vitebsk		
			9 Liakhovo	
		13 Aksentsy	13 Novo Shvershen, Mir	
		14 Smolyaentsy		
15	Dahlenkirchen	15 Kaydanovo		14–16 Volkovisk

Latvia	*North*	*Centre*	*South*
		17 Minsk	
		14–18 Krasnoy	
		21–23 Borisov	
		23 Chlopenitsche	
		24 Baturi	
		26–28 Beresina	

December
26   Piktupoenen

Bibliography

All sources listed are to be regarded as being at least 'good' regarding the relevance and detail of the information that they contain in relation to the study of the battle. Those that (in my opinion) exceed this 'basic' level have thus been classified as either: ★ for 'very good', or: ★★ for 'excellent'.

Adam, Albrecht, *Croquis Pittoresques Dessinés d'après Nature dans la Russie en 1812*, (Munich).

von Baden-Hochberg, Wilhelm, Markgraf, *Denkwürdigkeiten*, (Bearbeitet von Karl Obeser, Heidelberg, 1906).

von Barschewisch, Hauptmann, *Geschichte des Grossherzoglich Badischen Leib-Grenadier Regiments*, 1803–1871, (Karlsruhe, 1893).

★★Bogdanovich, Generalmajor M. I., *Geschichte des Feldzuges von 1812*, (Leipzig, 1863).

★★*Borodino 1812*, (Izdatelsvo Misl, Moscow, 1987).

Chandler, D. G., *The Campaigns of Napoleon*, (London, 1967).

★★Clausewitz, General Carl von, *The Campaign of 1812 in Russia*, (John Murray, London 1843; Greenhill, London 1992).

★★Clausewitz, Carl von, *Hinterlassene Werke*, vol.VII, *Der Feldzug 1812 in Russland*, (1843).

★von Ditfurth, Maximilian Freiherr, *Die Schlacht bei Borodino am 7 September 1812*, (Marburg, 1887).

★★Duffy, Christopher, *Borodino, Napoleon Against Russia, 1812*, (Sphere Books, London, 1972).

du Four, Faber, *Blätter aus Meinem Portefeul 1812*, (Leipzig, 1897).

George, Hereford, B., *The Moscow Expedition* (Oxford, 1904).

Gerdes, A. *Die Geschichte der Truppen Bergs und Westfalen 1812 in Russland*, (Langendreer, 1914).

Gerhardt, O, *Die Württemberger in Russland 1812*, (Stuttgart, 1937).

Heilmann, 'Die Bayerische Division Preysing im Feldzuge von 1812', in the *Jahrbuch für die Deutsche Armee und Marine*, vol. 17.

von Hohenhausen, Leopold, *Biographie des Générals von Ochs*, (Kassel, 1827).

★★Holzhausen, P, *Die Deutschen in Russland*, (Berlin, 1912).

von Kausler, Franz and Wörl, J. E., *Die Kriege von 1792–1815 in Europa und Ägypten mit Besondere Rücksicht auf die Schlachten Napoleons und seiner Zeit*, (Karlsruhe and Freiburg, 1842).

Kraft, Heinz, *Die Württemberger in den Napoleonischen Kriegen*, (Stuttgart, 1865).

Leyh, Max, *Die Feldzeuge des Königlich Bayerischen Heeres unter Max I Joseph von 1805 bis 1815.*

*von Lossberg, Friedrich, W., *Briefe in die Heimat Geschrieben Während des Feldzugs 1812 in Russland*, (Berlin, 1912).

**Lünsmann, Fritz, *Die Armee des Königsreichs Westfalen*, (Berlin, 1935).

Malibran, A. and Chelminski J., *L'Armée du Duche de Varsovie de 1807 à 1815*, (Paris, 1913).

**Morgenstern, Oberst Franz, *Kriegserinnerungen aus Westfälischer Zeit*, (Wolfenbüttel, 1912).

von Pivka, Otto, *Armies of 1812*, (PSL, Cambridge, 1977).

von Preysing-Moos, Generalmajor Maximilian, Graf, *Tagebuch 1812*, (Munich, 1912).

**Röder, Franz, *Der Kriegszug Napoleons Gegen Russland im Jahre 1812*, (Leipzig, 1848).

**von Roos, Heinrich, *Mit Napoleon in Russland*, (Stuttgart 1912).

**von Schreckenstein, Generalleutnant Roth, Freiherr, *Die Kavallerie in der Schlacht an der Moskva am 7 September 1812*, (Münster, 1855).

*von Schubert, F., *Unter dem Doppeladler: Erinnerungen eines Deutschen im Russischen Offiziersdienst 1789–1814*, (Stuttgart, 1962).

Smith, Digby, *The Greenhill Napoleonic Wars Data Book*, (Greenhill Books, London, 1998).

von Stein, F. *Geschichte des Russischen Heeres vom Ursprunge desselben bis zur Thronbesteigung des Kaisers Nikolai I*, (Pawlowitsch, Liepzig, 1895).

Thiers, Louis A., *The Moscow Expedition*, Oxford, 1904.

Tolstoy, Leo, *War and Peace.*

**von Wuerttemberg, Eugen, Herzog *Erinnerungen aus dem Feldzuge des Jahres 1812 in Russland*, (Breslau, 1846).

'Württemberger im Russischen Feldzug 1812', in *Württembergische Volksbücher*, (Stuttgart, 1911).

Index

GREAT BATTLES SERIES

HASTINGS
Peter Poyntz Wright
Paperback £9.99 Illustrated

AGINCOURT
Christopher Hibbert
Paperback £9.99 Illustrated

EDGEHILL: 1642
Peter Young
Paperback £15.99 Illustrated

MARSTON MOOR: 1644
Peter Young
Paperback £15.99 Illustrated

THE BATTLE OF THE BOYNE AND AUGHRIM:
THE WAR OF THE TWO KINGS
John Kinross
Paperback £10.99 Illustrated

CORUNNA
Christopher Hibbert
Paperback £12.99 Illustrated

WELLINGTON'S PENINSULAR VICTORIES
Michael Glover
Paperback £12.99 Illustrated

TRAFALGAR: THE NELSON TOUCH
David Howarth
Paperback £10.99 Illustrated

WATERLOO: A NEAR RUN THING
David Howarth
Paperback £12.99 Illustrated

ARNHEM
Christopher Hibbert
Paperback £10.99 Illustrated

Order from THE WINDRUSH PRESS, LITTLE WINDOW, HIGH
STREET, MORETON-IN-MARSH, GLOS. GL56 0LL
MAJOR CREDIT CARDS ACCEPTED
TEL: 01608 652012 FAX: 01608 652125
Please add £1 post and packing within the UK

MILITARY HISTORY BOOKS

THE LETTERS OF PRIVATE WHEELER 1809–1828
An eyewitness account of the Battle of Waterloo
Edited and with a foreword by B. H. Liddell Hart
'*Vivid images – of people, landscape, events – flow from his pen . . . one of military history's great originals*'
John Keegan
Paperback £9.99

THE DIARY OF A NAPOLEONIC FOOT SOLDIER
Jakob Walter
A conscript in the *Grande Armée*'s account of the long march home on the retreat from Moscow
Edited and Introduced by Mark Raeff
Paperback £9.99 Illustrated

THE RECOLLECTIONS OF RIFLEMAN HARRIS
One of the most popular military books of all time
Edited and Introduced by Christopher Hibbert
'*An ordinary soldier's memoirs are rare but precious. Harris's are a most vivid record of the war in Spain and Portugal against Napoleon, the same campaign as featured in the recent TV drama series, 'Sharpe'.*'
The Mail on Sunday
Paperback £9.99

THE RECOLLECTIONS OF SERGEANT MORRIS
These are among the liveliest and most revealing of that remarkable series of memoirs left by soldiers who fought against Napoleon
Edited by John Selby with an introduction by Peter Young
Paperback £9.99

A SOLDIER OF THE SEVENTY-FIRST
The journal of a Soldier in the Peninsular War
Edited and Introduced by Christopher Hibbert
'*His elegant style and his descriptive power take us with him at every step.*'
The Sunday Telegraph
Paperback £9.99

THE WHEATLEY DIARY
A Journal & Sketchbook from the Peninsular War &
The Waterloo Campaign
Edited and Introduced by Christopher Hibbert
Paperback £10.99 Illustrated in colour